ERIOS

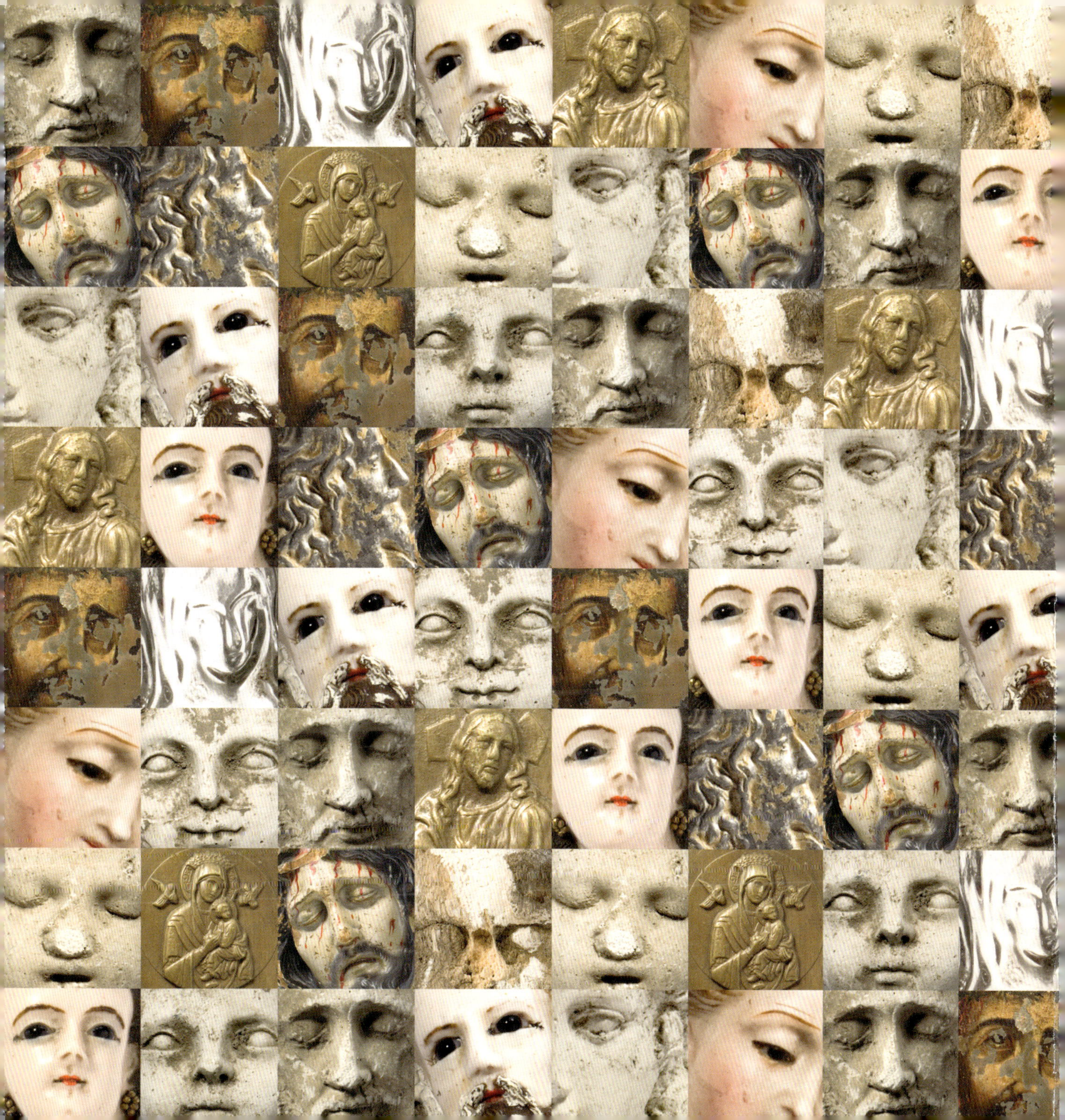

EDITED BY MIGUEL ANGEL CORZO

MISTERIOS

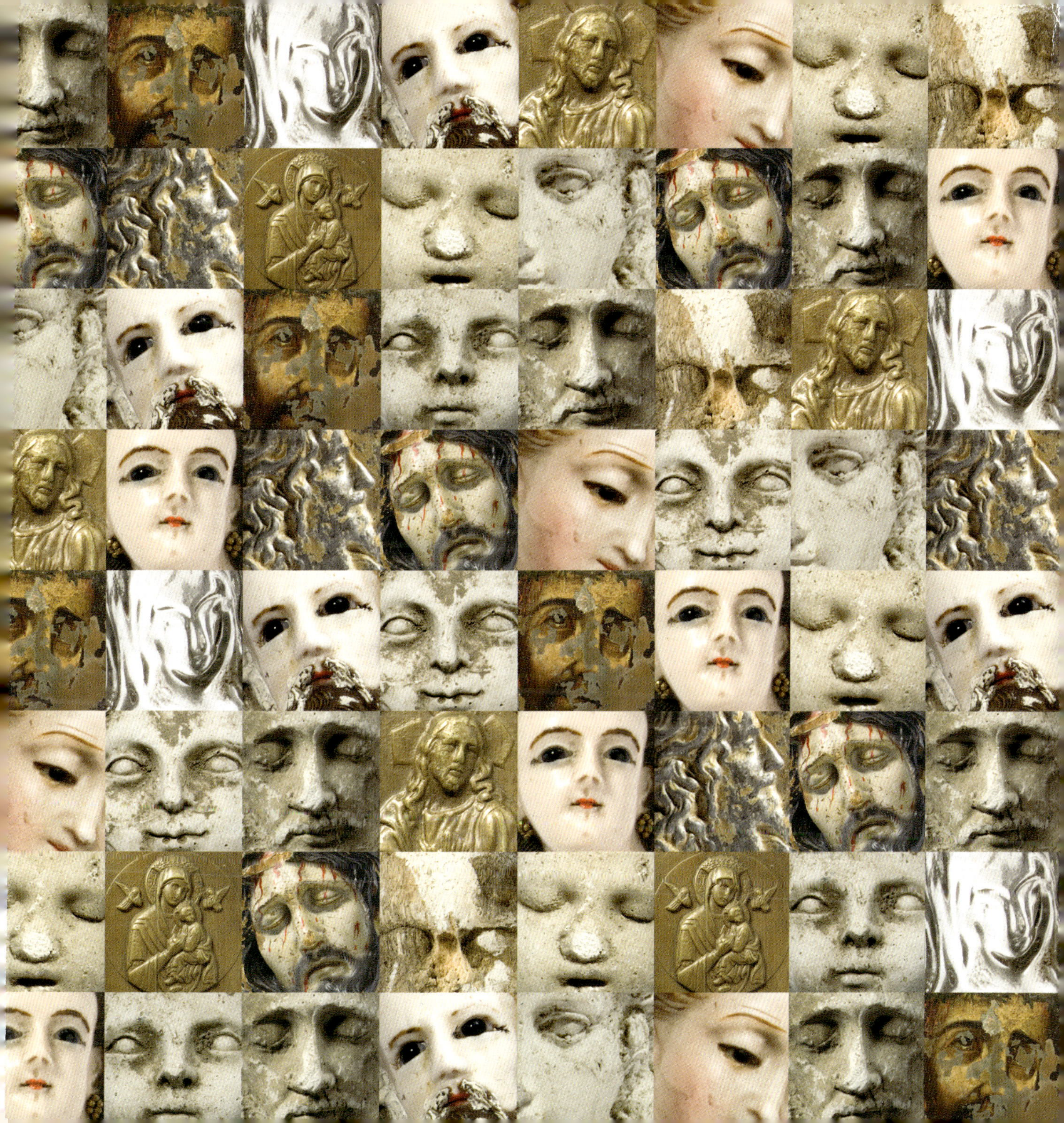

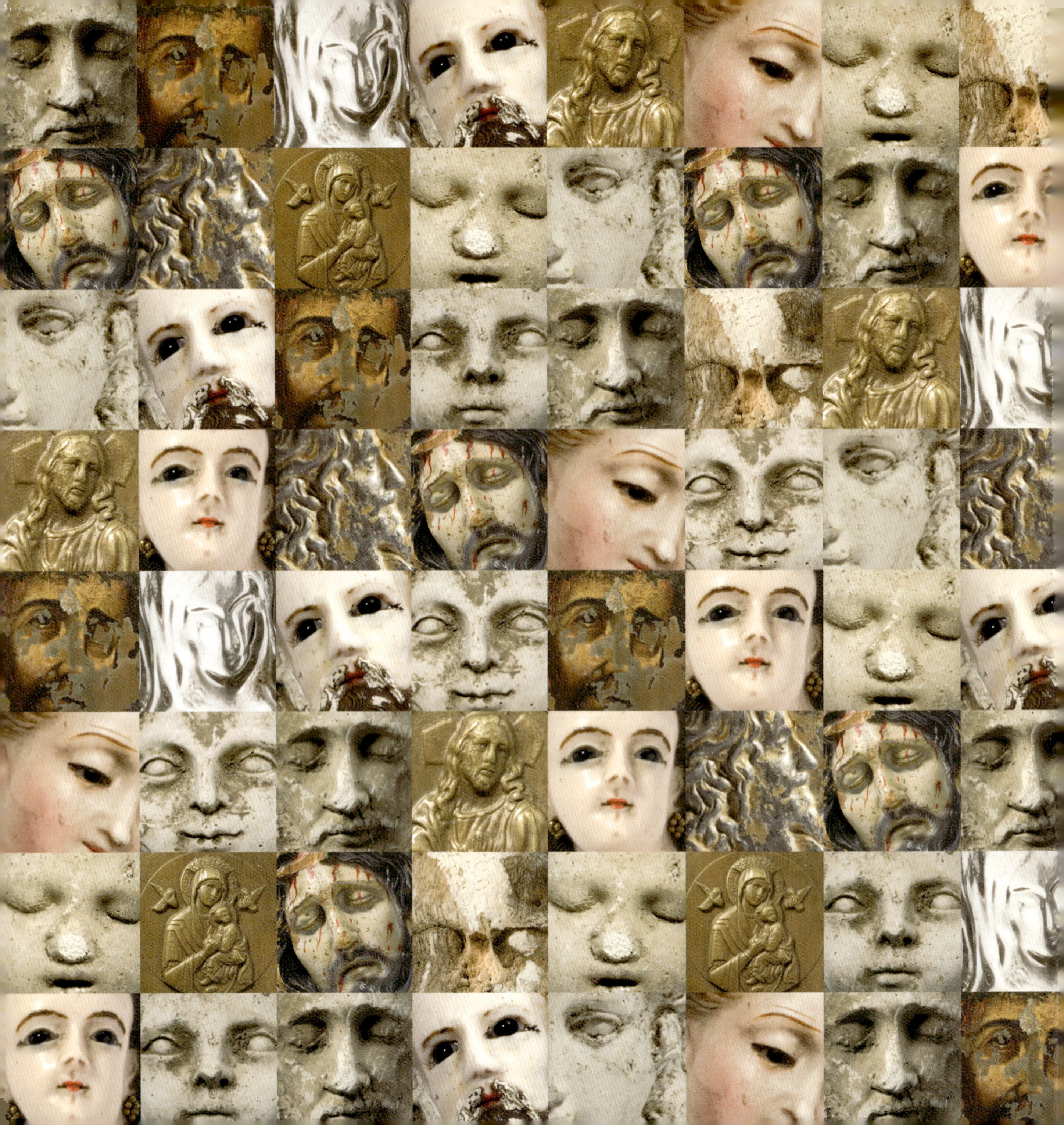

MISTERIOS

Miguel Angel Corzo
Sharon Church
Julián Zugazagoitia

Catalogue published on the occasion of the *Misterios* exhibition
The University of the Arts, Philadelphia, April 26, 2007
The Cathedral of the Saviour, Philadelphia, May 8 – May 27, 2007

Printed with pride by CRW Graphics in support of The University of the Arts.

Additional support for the exhibition comes from Harvey Kimmel in honor of Virginia Kimmel and Sharon Church, two inspiring people who love the crafts and care deeply about those who create them.

MISTERIOS: *an* EXTRAORDINARY EVOCATION *of the* CREATIVE IMPULSE *and the* PROFOUND ENIGMA *of* ART

Published by The University of the Arts

Copyright © 2007 by Miguel Angel Corzo & The University of the Arts.
All Rights reserved.

Published in the United States by The University of the Arts, Philadelphia, Pennsylvania
www.uarts.edu
The University of the Arts® is a registered trademark

Book Design by Mangos | mangosinc.com
Essay photographs by Guillermo Aldana
Artifact, student artwork and student portrait photographs by Ken Yanoviak

Corzo, Miguel Angel
Church, Sharon
Zugazagoitia, Julián
Misterios: an extraordinary evocation of the creative impulse and the profound enigma of art

ISBN 0-9617370-1-8

PRINTED IN THE UNITED STATES OF AMERICA
First Edition

Contents

002 Preface by Miguel Angel Corzo
004 Introduction by Sharon Church
007 Life, Religion and Art in Colonial Mexico by Miguel Angel Corzo
017 The Gift of Inspiration by Julián Zugazagoitia

023 Misterios

024 Angela C. Alberto
026 Martha A. Andrew
028 Ariel E. Axelrod-Hahn
031 Taryn L. Backus
032 Melody L. Basch
034 Marybeth E. Bent
038 Sarah A. Bernard
041 Emily R. Bixler
042 Chase M. Brown
044 Nina R. Brown
046 Chun Chun
049 Marianne E. Contreras
050 Christine Domanic
052 Desiree D. Fabela
056 William R. Fetzer
059 Amanda J. Foss
060 Katherine M. Fraser
062 Megan S. Frisch
064 Sara C. Gallo
067 Jennifer M. Gin
068 Genava L. Gisondi
070 Maximilian Greenberg
072 Lauren C. Gross
075 Erin E. Grunstra
078 Amanda L. Gutsche
080 Anna S. Ha
082 Elizabeth M. Henderson
085 Jessica L. Hersh
086 Beth-Ellen E. Hively
088 Sara Horne
090 Jenna R. Ilconich
093 Alexander P. Irvine
094 Matthew R. Kelso
096 Eleanor J. Kennell
100 Jillian A. Koehnken
103 Brittany A. Kurzweil
104 Lauren A. LeBlanc
106 Amanda L. Lewis
108 Colin J. Lusis
111 Andrea C. Manning
112 Margie M. Manogue
114 Emily R. Moroz
116 Jamie B. Newman
121 Jason T. O'Brien
122 Mary C. O'Malley
124 Amy L. Peseller
126 Joseph M. Pillari
129 Lauren P. Rider
130 Elizabeth K. Rogers
132 Shannon E. Ryan
134 Jason S. Saul
139 Margaret J. Schreiter
140 Michael J. Studebaker
142 Paola Tawa
144 Kirsten A. Teel
147 Chia-Wei Ting
150 Stephanie L. Tomczak
152 Marcy Vanderburg
154 Kort A. Walsh
157 Christopher N. Yoos
158 Lindsey A. Zmroczek

160 Faculty

"The most beautiful thing we can experience is the mysterious. It is the source of all true art and all science. He to whom this emotion is a stranger, who can no longer pause to wonder and stand rapt in awe, is as good as dead: his eyes are closed."

ALBERT EINSTEIN

Preface

Misterios is a window to the imagination and the creativity of a dedicated group of students from The University of the Arts, guided by a caring and superb faculty led by Professors Sharon Church and Rod McCormick.

The genesis of *Misterios* came about when my good friend, Joe Rischel, talked to me for the first time about the *Tesoros* exhibition that he was organizing at the Philadelphia Museum of Art. I was excited by the exceptional opportunity the exhibit afforded our students to see examples of a very special period of Latin American art. They would be able to experience first hand extraordinary objects of profound historic and artistic value of the colonial era of Latin America.

Having been a witness to the exceptional results of a previous project, where students took disparate objects assembled through world travels and turned them into magnificent artistic objects, I felt this was a new opportunity. Why not, I asked Professors Sharon Church and Rod McCormick, bring some religious objects from Mexico and have a new group of students attempt another project? My colleagues generously and enthusiastically approached the idea and involved other faculty members of The University of the Arts as well as a large number of students.

Faced with the need to gather these objects, I enrolled more friends in the project. Through the help of certainly the two best art restorers in Latin America, Agustín and Cecilia Espinosa, we were able to obtain various religious objects in Mexico. Their daughter, UArts senior in Music Natalia Espinosa, brought the first batch during a trip home. My friend and cultural accomplice of many years, Rosalía Navarro, brought the second batch. And when we all gathered to see them, we were seduced by their richness. These were objects that UArts students would be able to study, be inspired by, and then interpret or transform. The result of the project is a magnificent display of incredible power and creativity.

Professors Church and McCormick have my continuous gratitude for their amazing dedication and teaching skills. I would particularly like to thank my friend and colleague, Julián Zugazagoitia, for writing a magnificent essay on the crafts. The exhibition would also not have been possible without the dedication, diplomacy and tenacity of Saba Rodriguez and her staff. Karen Rosenberg and Kelly Fernández brought their organizational skills and their enthusiasm to the project. Riyehee Hong, Director of Music and Art at the Cathedral of the Saviour in Philadelphia, generously offered the use of that magnificent venue to extend the exhibition. My sincere gratitude to all. And to the UArts students my admiration for their extraordinary abilities and profound insights.

To many the creative process is a mystery, a combination of circumstances, including the shaping of ideas and materials and the tenacity of young and curious minds, which can result in an exhibition as magnificent as *Misterios*. I am sure you will delight in unraveling its enigmas.

MIGUEL ANGEL CORZO
President and CEO
The University of the Arts

Introduction

In Fall of 2006, The Philadelphia Museum of Art opened its blockbuster show, *Tesoros/Treasures/Tesouros: The Arts in Latin America, 1492–1820*. The works in that exhibition were created in the aftermath of the colonization of Mexico and Latin America by Spain and Portugal, when two radically different worlds collided. The swift fall of the Aztec Empire and the rapid conversion of the remaining native culture to Catholicism that followed colonization were all reflected in works which embodied the unique culture that emerged from that period of conflict.

The show presented a singular opportunity that Miguel Angel Corzo, President of UArts, seized upon. He assembled a collection of 20 Colonial Mexican artifacts and presented them to the Crafts Department. What might UArts Crafts students create if they were given Colonial Mexican artifacts to use in their own work? How would they, as contemporary artists, respond to objects made several hundred years ago? How would they interpret and employ these objects, especially when viewed against the backdrop of the *Tesoros* exhibition? How would their work bridge the gap between two cultures—Colonial Latin American and contemporary American society?

This was an exceptional educational challenge for our students: to reach beyond the University to the Museum and to a centuries old culture through their own creative work.

Each student was presented with options about how to proceed. Using our 3-D laser scanner and Perfactory 3-D printer, we created digital replicas of the artifacts and printed them out in acrylic plastic. Some students had these plastic replicas to use, others worked directly with the objects themselves, and others simply worked with the ideas and concepts behind them.

Whichever methodology a student chose, the challenge was to develop a work of art that offered his or her unique interpretation of a specific colonial artifact. Students studied the works at the Museum, pored through books and catalogues, examined the history of the colonization of Latin America and were enthralled with Miguel Angel's lecture on México Barroco. They worked long and hard on their project, returning during their winter break to bring their work to successful conclusion.

Across the board, our students extended beyond their previous capacities to create *Misterios*: an extraordinary evocation of the creative impulse and the profound enigma of art.

SHARON CHURCH
Director, Crafts

Retablos, *intricately carved from wood or plaster, are interior facades in Latin American colonial churches, above the main altar in chapels. Profusely gilded and lavishly decorated, the niches held figures of Christ, the Virgin or various saints. They were conceived to astonish the believers with the power and the majesty of the images.*

Life, Religion and Art in Colonial Mexico

Nobel laureate in Literature Octavio Paz said that "the will to create has never floundered in 40 centuries in Mexico." Colonial Mexican art is certainly part of that will. The European presence in Mexico created a set of attitudes and artistic manifestations that spread throughout the country and beyond with an astonishing diversity of expressions and nuances.

The conquest of the Americas was driven by religion and by creed. Once urban centers were established, the crown and the Spanish settlers immediately launched an intensive effort to "civilize" the indigenous people. Little by little, the native inhabitants were converted to the Christian faith and compelled to live in a "civilized" manner so that their social and economic structures could be adapted and modified for the benefit of the Spanish and the colonial system.[1]

According to Bernal Diaz del Castillo, the soldier and chronicler who accompanied Hernán Cortez on his conquest of Mexico, the Emperor Montezuma received the Spaniards in Tenochtitlan, the capital city of the Aztec Empire and 30 times larger than Seville whence Cortez came. After he installed them in the palaces that had belonged to his father, Axayácatl, Cortez made a request for masons, "so that we can make a church in our lodgings. And in three days our church was made. And once it was finished we were daily in the church praying on our knees before the altar and images." This took place in 1521. The extraordinary dexterity of the builders and stonemasons of ancient Mexico was a natural resource the Spaniards could readily employ to achieve their political and religious designs.[2]

Sacred Spaces

The Catholic papacy selected mendicant friars—Franciscans, Dominicans and Augustinians—to carry the thrust of evangelization in New Spain because of their missionary zeal and vows of poverty.[3] The first major group to arrive was a cohort of twelve Franciscans in 1524, followed two years later by twelve Dominicans, and in 1533 by seven Augustinians. The native Mexicans recognized these friars as similar to their own priests, who lived equally chaste and austere lives, and they seemed willing to accept the Spanish supernaturals without much argument, just as they had earlier added the gods of their indigenous neighbors to their own pantheons. A powerful alliance was forged between the indigenous populations and the mendicant friars charged with their conversion that continues to this day.

Under the oversight of the friars, native artists learned the European formal canons and religious iconography, copying compositions directly from graphic images, especially prints that arrived from Europe, or drawing on them more directly for inspiration and imagery. Mural programs painted almost entirely in European style on the walls of the churches, chapels and cloisters, carried Christian messages to both mendicants and natives who equally understood the didactic power of the images.[4]

In addition to the master builders, architects, masons, and stonecutters directly responsible for the architectural structures, each of these buildings required the collaboration of cabinetmakers, cartwrights, woodworkers, engravers and joiners in charge of the altarpieces, stalls, pulpits and altars—not to mention the more ordinary furnishings.[5] There were goldsmiths and silversmiths who produced the tabernacles, chalices, ciboria, patens, incense burners, cruets, sacrine tablets, candlesticks, sacrariums and

The wide variety of figures required tremendous care. Wood polychrome sculptures, with lifelike faces in flesh tones, provided a connection to the stories of the life or the miracles performed by the saints and the archangels who protect the image of the Virgin.

Archangels, saints and martyrs, in the middle of abundant foliages or flowers, represent a visual hymn to the passion and martyrdom of the Son of God. Tonantzintla chapel in Puebla, Mexico.

monstrances, lecterns, reliquaries, coffers, lamps, crosses, and even altar frontals for entire altarpieces, as well as the plentiful jewelry that adorned the images for the prelates themselves, encrusted with gemstones cut by the lapidaries. There were the makers of violas, organs, and other musical instruments, and the miniaturists who illustrated the psalters.

Stone sculptures adorned the exteriors of churches and cathedrals, and large outdoor stone crosses, infused with indigenous forms and styles, were among the most important works of early colonial art. Sculptors and painters also produced the statues, panels and canvases that formed part of the *retablos* or altarpieces, or decorated the walls of naves, sacristies, chapter houses, and other internal departments of the cathedrals. Gilders and *encarnadores* (painters of flesh tones of sculptures) provided color for these images and for the altarpieces themselves while ironworkers and locksmiths fashioned grilles and gates.[6]

Ultimately, the architectural features of the religious complexes they created met the special requirements of their society: open chapels and large *atrios* or patios accommodated great numbers of Christian worshippers who were previously accustomed to open air religious observances of their own gods.[7]

A Unifying Force
As the population of Mexico grew, social life needed to be organized through legal norms. Each one of these norms was directed to a sector of the population, be they Spaniards, Indians, or individuals of mixed blood. As a result, the unity of the country was in jeopardy. The church seized the opportunity to present itself as the unifying institution for the country. While the state, through codes and laws divided the population, the church assembled this complex society. This is the reason for the extraordinary significance of the churches as a unifying social force. In addition, the level of illiteracy remained high throughout the colonial period, which meant church dogma was taught primarily through sermons and images. As a result, the birth and development of colonial or vice-regal art was intimately linked with the teaching of Christian doctrine.[8]

The opulence of the churches themselves was designed to impress the faithful, and by extension, other religious congregations, which naturally sparked the urge to emulate the Catholic example. All types of objects dramatically transformed the interior spaces of churches and also flaunted their wealth, attesting to the huge economic power that lay behind each congregation.

Many of the *retablos* were conceived for young seminarians, to marvel and astonish the teenagers who wanted to become active Jesuits. Façades showed complex patterned surfaces; the columns were decorated with a variety of contrasting, highly unclassical geometric designs, with figures carved at the bases of the columns, the Virgin often flanked by monumental figures of saints standing stiffly in their niches. There were profusions of figures in the overall form of an altarpiece with niches and clearly demarcated stories, richly carved with foliate and vegetal decoration and peopled by slightly awkward, stumpy figures.

Convents and churches show exceptional retablos *starting at the presbytery. The work is done by native Mexicans directed by the Spanish priests or builders. The wealth of the Church imposed a heavy burden on the population by exacting a continuous demand for the construction of scenes of overwhelming luxury.*

The mother of Christ holding the body of her son, surrounded by ornamental excesses, evokes profound feelings. The passion, the exuberance of details and the artistic elements are geared to exalt the religious feelings of the believer. Ocotlán church, Tlaxcala, Mexico.

The church also took advantage of its fundamental role by teaching singing, reading and writing. In many cases this instruction was expanded to include various trades, such as building construction, the fabrication of musical instruments, and the fine arts of painting and sculpture, all in the service of religious worship.

Spiritual Expressions
In its protagonist role, the church encouraged the active participation and collective expression of indigenous people and *mestizos* through religious celebrations, masquerades, fireworks, bullfights, and religious processions. The emphasis was on integration. The capacity to appropriate ideas, concepts, and forms was not linear, but rather enveloping and creative, generating new responses.

The profound piety of every stratum of colonial society meant that through various mechanisms, a good part of the colony's profits were funneled into the church and into religious ritual. In a world where religion accompanied a human being from cradle to grave, where all ceremonies, whether of transcendent or secondary importance were marked by the presence of church, it is not surprising that society devoted itself to serving God and his representatives on earth. Even today, religious fiestas are so magnificent that people pay to see the processions. In the *Gazetas de México*, all the news related to these events are described: the opening of the *retablo*, the fiesta of such and such saint, the procession in such and such city.

Different from what was happening in some parts of Europe, we can see in New Spain a rich, flowery and spontaneous presence; there is a relationship between the visual feelings of the Mexican and the popular life of their common manifestations. Mexico was a world of fiestas, of processions, of triumphal arches, of symbolic publicity, of verbal games, of wonders, illusions, pessimism, melancholy, executions, torments and misleading presences. It was the home of painters, poets, geniuses, Don Juanes, mystics, dwarfs, insane individuals, homeless, dandies, all of whom created a unique human panorama.

The indigenous populations reflect with great care the spirit and the sensitivity of their creators. This is a world that informs and astonishes. This desire to want to be permanently in contact with God is justified because it talks about divine omnipresence. Time and space belong to the church. In the city invaded by temples and in the year invaded by fiestas, the New Spaniard seems to occupy his life in religious activities.

The sculptures of saints, the Virgin or Christ are luxuriously dressed to reflect the liturgical calendar. Some of the figures are used in processions on holy feasts and the villagers elect the dressers and the bearers of the statues as a symbol of standing in the community.

Time is measured in credos or in prayers which is fantastic, surrealist and timeless. The Creole, the Spaniards born in New Spain, participate in the need to increase the court of the king of heaven, with the idea that God is everywhere and in everything. The Creole assumes that he can be seen, spoken to, and therefore feels God is constantly in his environment. Novenas, for example, were prayers that served everything. There were novenas for good respect or novenas for storms or for impossible deeds or for epilepsy or for pestilence and there were novenas to be protected against thieves and some to professed sins that were held inside because of shame. Diseases were also cured with novenas; it was believed that the prayers solved everything.[9]

A Manifestation of Identity
The Spanish Empire founded close to a thousand cities over its nearly three centuries of colonial domination of the Americas. These cities functioned as grand arenas of social interactions, as well as administrative and religious centers par excellence, loci for the diffusion of culture and education, settings for multiple political and social events, and junctions in the complex trade networks, among many other roles.[10]

The Spanish environment of the 17th and the 18th centuries was characterized by intolerance and religiosity, by grandeur and decadence, by gentlemanliness and lasciviousness, by insolence and submission, by carnality and aestheticism. That is to say, it is a vast repertory of attitudes and of contradictory and disproportionate human beings. Society itself lacks equilibrium and is polarized. Eccentricities, extravagances, excesses, exaggerations and extremes prevail and the means and the appearances are more important than the ends and the functions.[11]

The individual in this baroque period is most of all an eccentric, an exaggeration. He becomes astonished by everything. He is horrified by everything. He sees what the average reasonable human being cannot see. He understands what is apparent, what is illusory, what is fictitious and his life is like a dream, only to be awakened by death. The other extreme is a hyper-realism that penetrates reality in a cool, mocking or ruthless way.

Form imposes over the idea; impression imposes on reflection, and the attempt to persuade through the emotions, the senses and the forms becomes an acrobatic experience. It also reveals the projection of a state of being that refuses nothing. What is festive and what is flowery do not eliminate what the ultimate goal is. Material realization brings with it the spiritual message.

The art of Colonial Latin America is a manifestation that represents the spirit of the whole people. Its rich visual content and the historic moment in which it arises reflect artistic social and cultural traditions where each painting and each monument are discovered and identified spiritually. In a final analysis, it is an expression of a human attitude and of a disproportionate reality that reflects some of the deeper currents of the creation of the national identity of Mexicans, which is as complex as it is passionate. This is the setting for the *Misterios* project.

What the students of The University of the Arts have accomplished through their work is nothing short of amazing. Through their work they have created an image of the past that becomes a source of a clearer perception of the present.

MIGUEL ANGEL CORZO

Painted images, by the most noted artists, were often used in the retablos *to represent passages of the bible and to be used as illustrations for the catechism. The combination of various visual arts brought many craftsmen and artists to New Spain, to the extent that at times, their immigration from Europe was prohibited.*

Notes

1. Alfonso Ortiz Crespo. *The Spanish American Colonial City* in "The Arts in Latin America 1492–1820." Philadelphia Museum of Art 2006.

2. M. Concepción García Saíz. *Artisans and Artists in Ibero-America from the Sixteenth to the Eighteenth Century* in "The Arts in Latin America 1492–1820." Philadelphia Museum of Art 2006.

3. Elizabeth Hill Boone and Thomas B.F. Cummins. *Colonial Foundations: Points of Contact and Compatibility* in "The Arts in Latin America 1492–1820." Philadelphia Museum of Art 2006.

4. Ibid.

5. García Saíz. Ibid.

6. García Saíz. Ibid.

7. Hill and Cummins. Ibid.

8. Guillermo Tovar de Teresa. *México Barroco*. SAHOP. Mexico 1981.

9. Ibid.

10. Ortiz Crespo. Ibid.

11. Tovar de Teresa. Ibid.

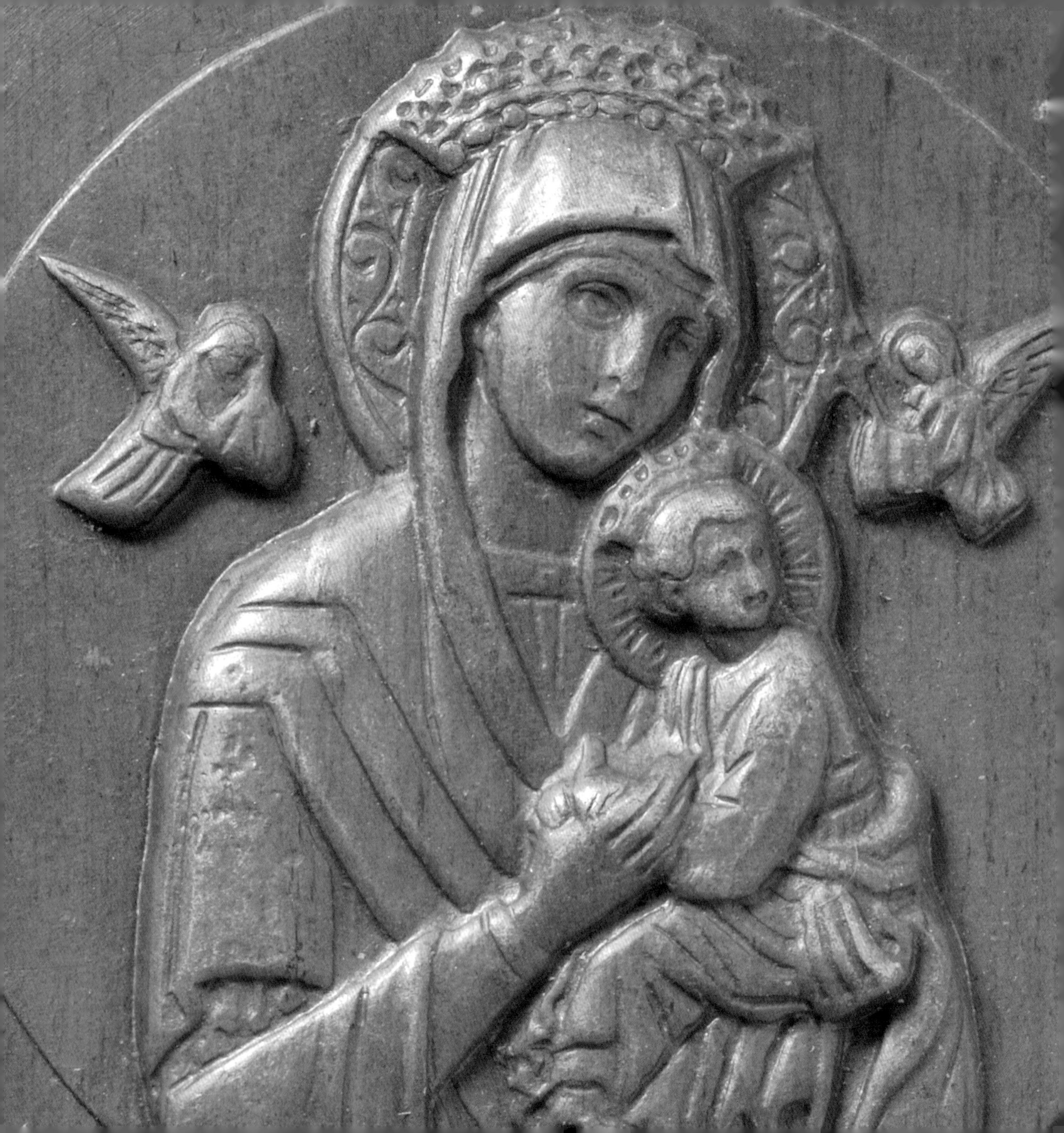

The Gift
of Inspiration

The *Misterios* Crafts project has produced an exhibit of extraordinary impact and inspiration. The pieces produced by the University of the Arts students are a testimony to their great creativity, and to the role of a commission as a way to expand one's horizon. In designing this project, I recognize Miguel Angel Corzo's constant desire to enrich people's lives with a deeper understanding and participation in the arts. This exercise began with a visit to the lavish exhibition, *Tesoros: The Arts in Latin America, 1492–1820,* at the Philadelphia Museum of Art. The students were then were offered objects from Mexico ranging from contemporary Milagritos to fragments of antique religious artifacts, which placed these young and talented artists in a very unique position—that of addressing a commission and approaching their creativity from a particular perspective.

The quality of the pieces that have resulted and the artists' statements indicate clearly the transformative nature of this project. Certainly the superlative quality of the survey of colonial art left a mark on them, but I want to believe that the impact would not have been as deep if these artists had not seen it with the perspective of being inspired by it. Their disposition was not that of passively visiting the galleries, but that of an inquisitive enjoyment with views to their own practice.

The demand for religious objects was such that manufacturing processes had to be devised to satisfy it. The objects were also given as favor by the religious orders or sold to benefit the church and to be worn as talismans for protection. Die-stamped figurines were particularly popular.

Naturally, for artists like these students who are versatile in all the crafts, *Tesoros* was an ideal ground. It presented works in all media, from silversmith to wood carving, from cabinet making to textiles, feathers, painting and lacquers. I imagine them surprised by the exuberance of many of these objects, by the lavish use of materials, by the opulence of the times and remote locations from which they came from. Those treasures bring to light the great craftsmanship that existed then, and they reinforce how some of those traditions have been lost forever.

For some of the students, the assignment triggered the idea of reviving some of those crafts. For others, they were inspired to interpret what once was, and adapt it to a digital world. For all it was an intense visit—looking as a way of probing each work. How was it made? What does it mean? How would they have created it? What is its meaning to their own practice?

The charged historical dimension of many of the pieces is reflected in their artistic interpretation. From today's highly secular, contemporary world, *Tesoros* opened the door to a civilization that was highly structured and dominated by the Christian faith. The religious themes that dominated much of the presentation revived in these young artists many intense feelings. For some, it was a reminder of family traditions. For others, their rejection of those practices. For some of the students it was a religious narrative foreign to their own background. But for all of them the exhibition and its subject matter triggered a profound dialogue between the works and their own understanding of artistic practices around the world.

The level of craftsmanship developed in Colonial times in Latin America reached astonishing quality. Heads made of porcelain with glass eyes were produced with lifelike, vibrant character, to be used in wooden body frames that would then be dressed to adorn home altars.

Plaster casts of cherubs and angels were particularly cherished for many celebrations, including the adornment of Nativity scenes or as faces of Child Jesus. The plaster was painted to lifelike quality, always representing a white angel, except in very unusual circumstances.

The experience of the exhibition was further heightened by the gift of the objects that they were given to incorporate into their own creation. The objects were a catalyst and a mediator: a catalyst that brought the ideas from the exhibition to their present realization, and a mediator between their formal stylistic practices and that of the donated object and its symbolic religious universe. The results of these commissions are extraordinary. In each what comes to light is the unique personality of the artists. What prevails is the sense that the past becomes alive. Through the use of found artifacts charged with their own history, activated by the understanding and inspiration of a superlative exhibition, they are transformed by the unique artistic sensibility of each of the students into a contemporary work of art.

This commission certainly expanded the realm of questions that the students were dealing with, and what appeared at the beginning a challenge or a constraint, ended up being a revelation for them as well as for all of us. In a way, what we are given to see is how thematically selected works of art, gathered temporarily at a museum, spark the imagination of contemporary artists and transform their production into something unexpected. The power of art is that of traveling generations and maintaining their quality of awe. Something of the 18th century craftsman is passed along the way to these young artists. The works in this catalogue are thus a vehicle to past *Tesoros* and bridge to newer ones still.

020 MISTERIOS

Despite their individuality and their differences, stylistically, technically and even in conceptual approach, what each of these pieces has in common is that they are inspired. It might seem an old fashioned word—inspired, or belonging to a kind of critical discourse no longer in use—yet that is what is clearly underlying each of these works. And if I resort to that notion I find that inspiration is the signature way in which Miguel Angel Corzo affects change in people's lives. I do not know how these young artists will remember this commission in many years, but I believe that they will never see an exhibition, regardless of its theme or nature, without engaging their entire self, without contemplating what, in their own practice, is triggered by what they have in front of them. They expanded their horizons by attacking a subject that was not among their immediate preoccupations, and in a way enriched their vocabulary. The students were forced to find within themselves something that had not reveled itself to them before.

With this commission, President Corzo was doing what he enjoys most: sharing his passion for the arts, cultures and history; but above all, engaging others with the arts in a way that they are transformed. These qualities transcend those of the educator that he has always been. What I have always valued (and this project is just one of many examples) is his unique way to inspire people to become more of themselves. Here we have the expression of 61 artists that have been inspired and are expressing their talent with these works that reinterpret the past and inform the future. Each, in its own way, is a tribute to Miguel Angel Corzo's gift to inspire.

JULIAN ZUGAZAGOITIA
Director
El Museo, New York

Wood sculptures of saints or of Christ during his Passion reached remarkable levels of artistic quality. Skilled wood carvers would be sought after to produce these statues for churches, oratories or home altars. Many would be carefully polychromed to show the anguish and the pain as well as the serenity of Jesus in his final moments.

Frames for images of the various representations of the Virgin or figures of saints were highly valued and created in different metals to enhance the value of the ornament. This photo shows the stamp of the silversmith guaranteeing the purity of the silver as .925 Sterling, the highest level.

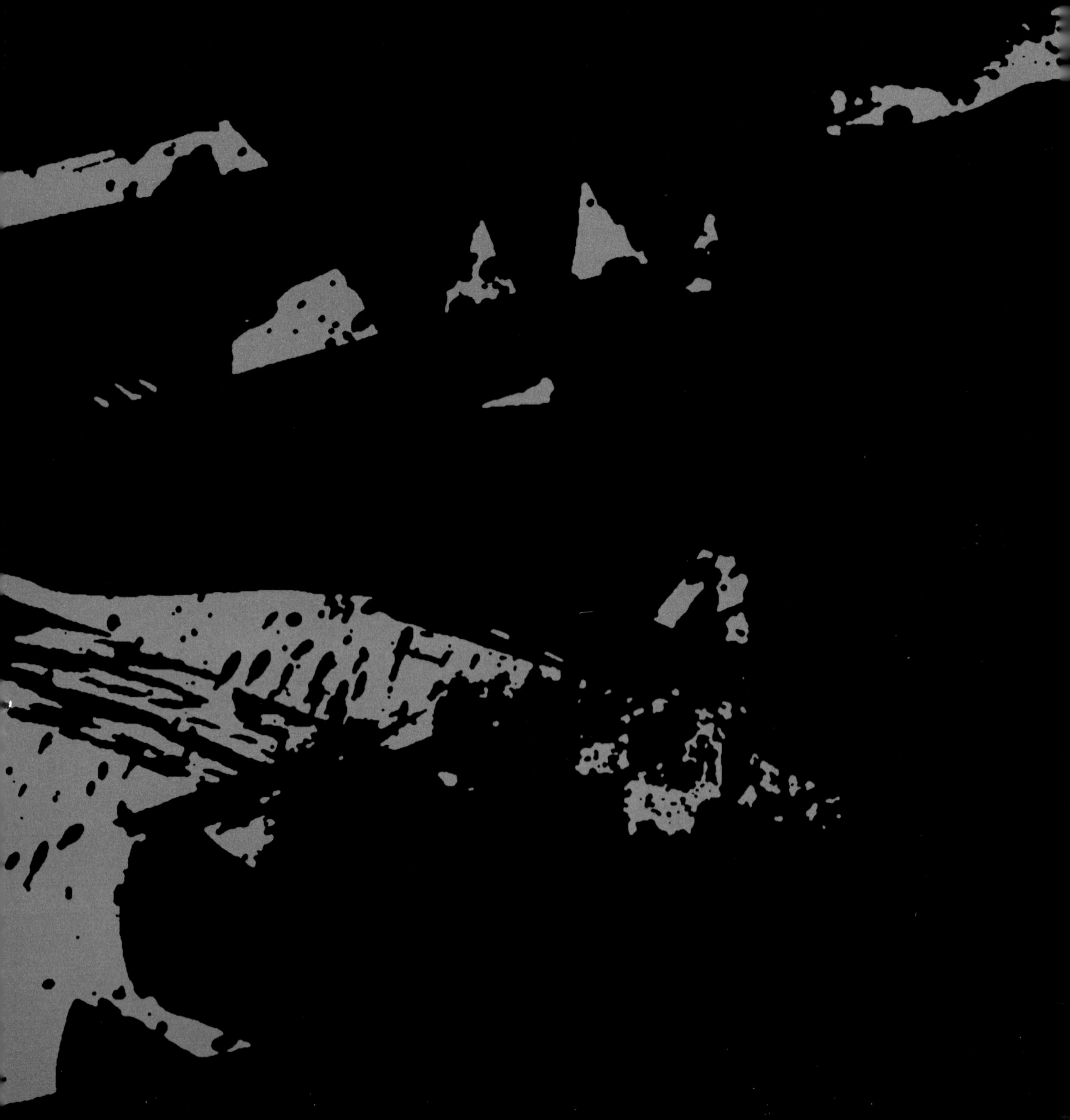

MISTERIOS

024 MISTERIOS

When I began working on the *Misterios* project, I was mourning the death of my uncle. I began to create a stained glass window as a memorial to him—a symbolic landscape that included portraits of both my aunt and uncle. A few days before the project was due, the largest piece of glass made for the sky broke in half. I was devastated. I had no money, or time, to remake that piece. I also realized that there was much about the design that I was not satisfied with. After I got over my devastation, I began to assemble those pieces of glass that were most appealing to me. I developed a window that not only involved my glass skills, but my metal working abilities as well. Until that piece broke, I had kept my work in metal and glass separate. Now I am working on a new path, combining two materials that have always excited me.

Angela C. Alberto

You Are Going To Go Far (2006)

Flash Glass
Copper
Lead
10″ x 10″

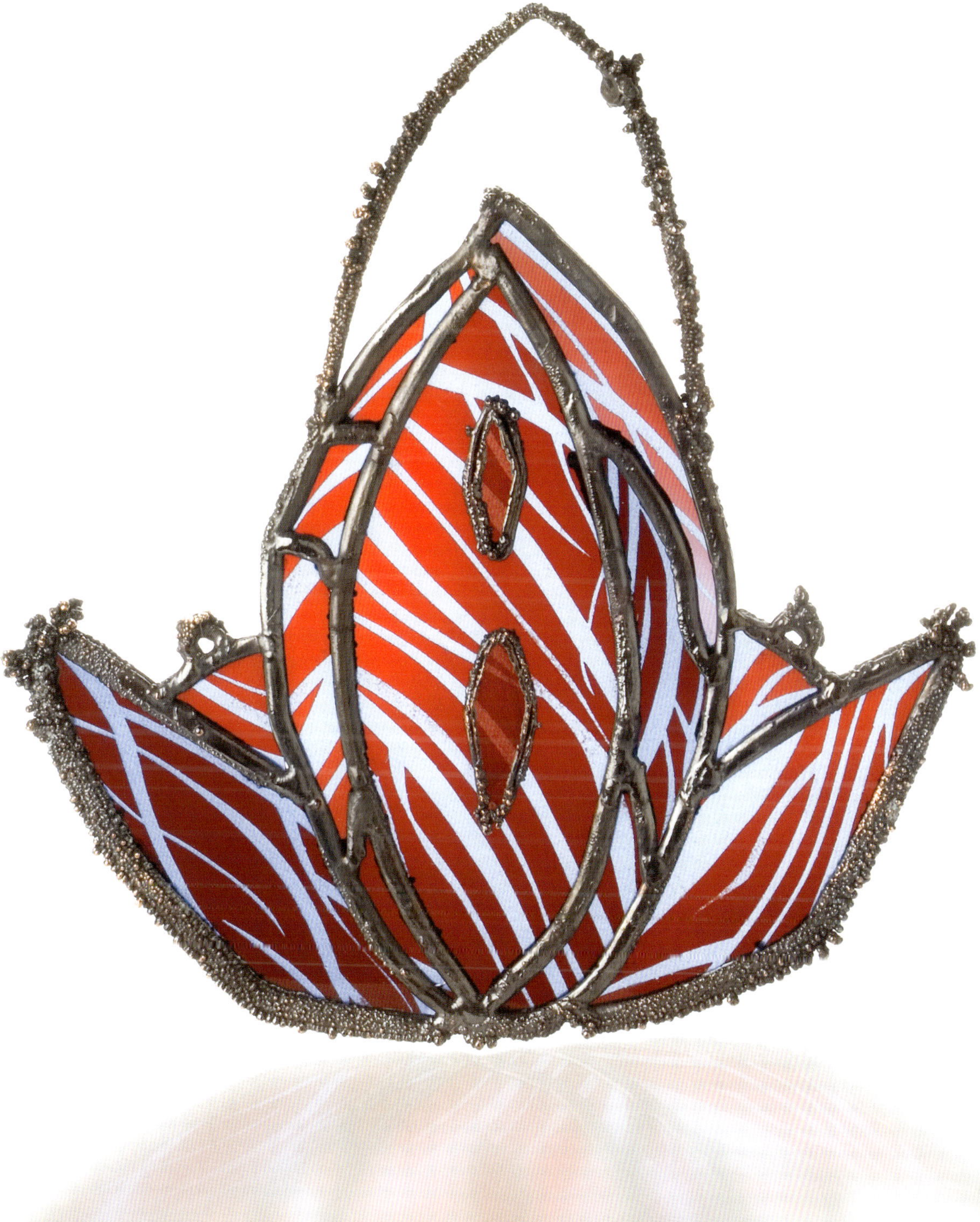

026 MISTERIOS

War and Religion.

Martha A. Andrew

War and Religion (2007)

Sterling Silver
Bronze
3" x 3" x 1"

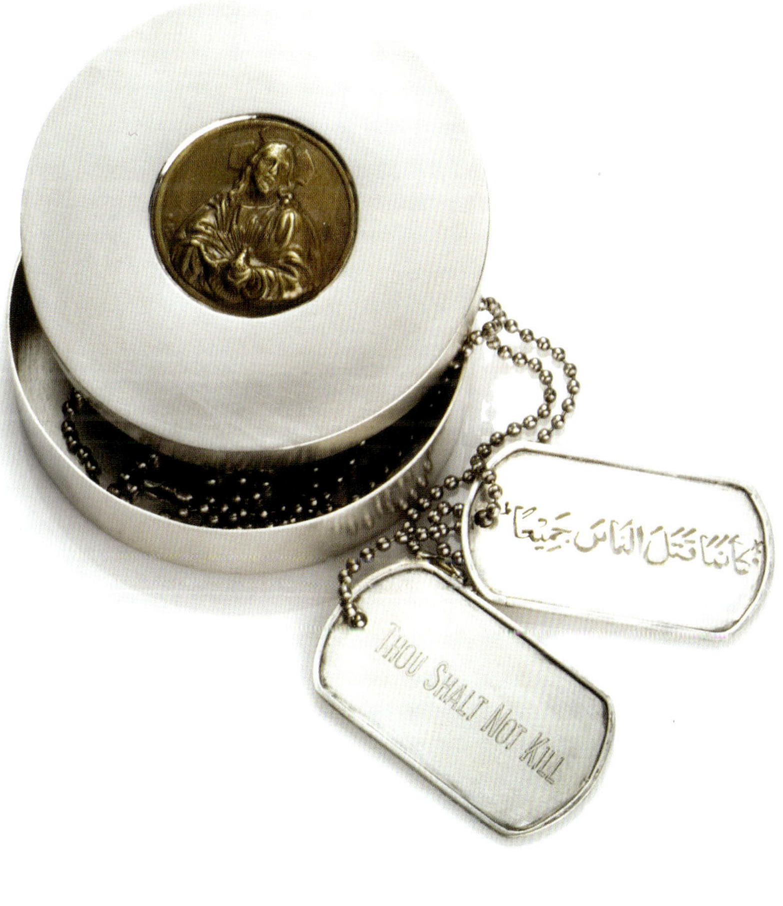
كانما قتل الناس جميعا
Thou Shalt Not Kill

Ariel E. Axelrod-Hahn

Erola and Aphelia (2007)

High-Fired Glazed Stoneware
12″ x 30″ x 10″

I used a figurine-sized bust of a woman as the focus for my *Misterios* piece. Although I did not physically incorporate the bust into my work, it did lead me to concentrate on the body rather than the religious aspects of the assignment. I was heavily influenced by the work of the *Tesoros* exhibition, especially those paintings which juxtaposed written evocations and supporting imagery. I ultimately chose the bust because it provided me with the widest range of plausible reactions to the *Tesoros* show.

Two pictures from the museum stand out in my mind as especially influential: the first was a diptych of two men confessing to priests. One was thoroughly engrossed in the act of penitence while the other paid only half a mind to his remorse. A priest smiled down at the first, while the second priest frowned at the demons hanging in the shadows behind the unrepentant man. The two frames were connected by several phrases floating over both scenes, imploring the audience to be honest and sincere in their atonement, lest they too suffer the lesser man's demon-filled fate.

Another piece that had a strong impact on me was a large painting of two martyred priests—thin and unblemished—save for a ring of blood dripping from each man's neck. The blood hung on the skin ornamentally, and, where it dripped on their frocks, it appeared to leave no stain. Both men simply stood and smiled out from the picture plane, neither betraying the pain that must have accompanied such wounds. They wore death like accoutrement, something distant and apart from their lives that must have ended rather abruptly. It was these two works that led me to challenge myself: could I depict a person's emotionally ruinous state through his physical state?

I have always brought some form of erosion into my work. In the two aforementioned paintings, the *Tesoros* artists dehumanized both saint and sinner, ignoring the inevitable erosion of their subjects' human dignity that would have resulted from the physical pain of martyrdom or the spiritual pain of damnation. In my own work, I would like to present what is missing from much of the *Tesoros* work; I wish to reverse this eradication of emotion and physical sensation from what must have been a painful end.

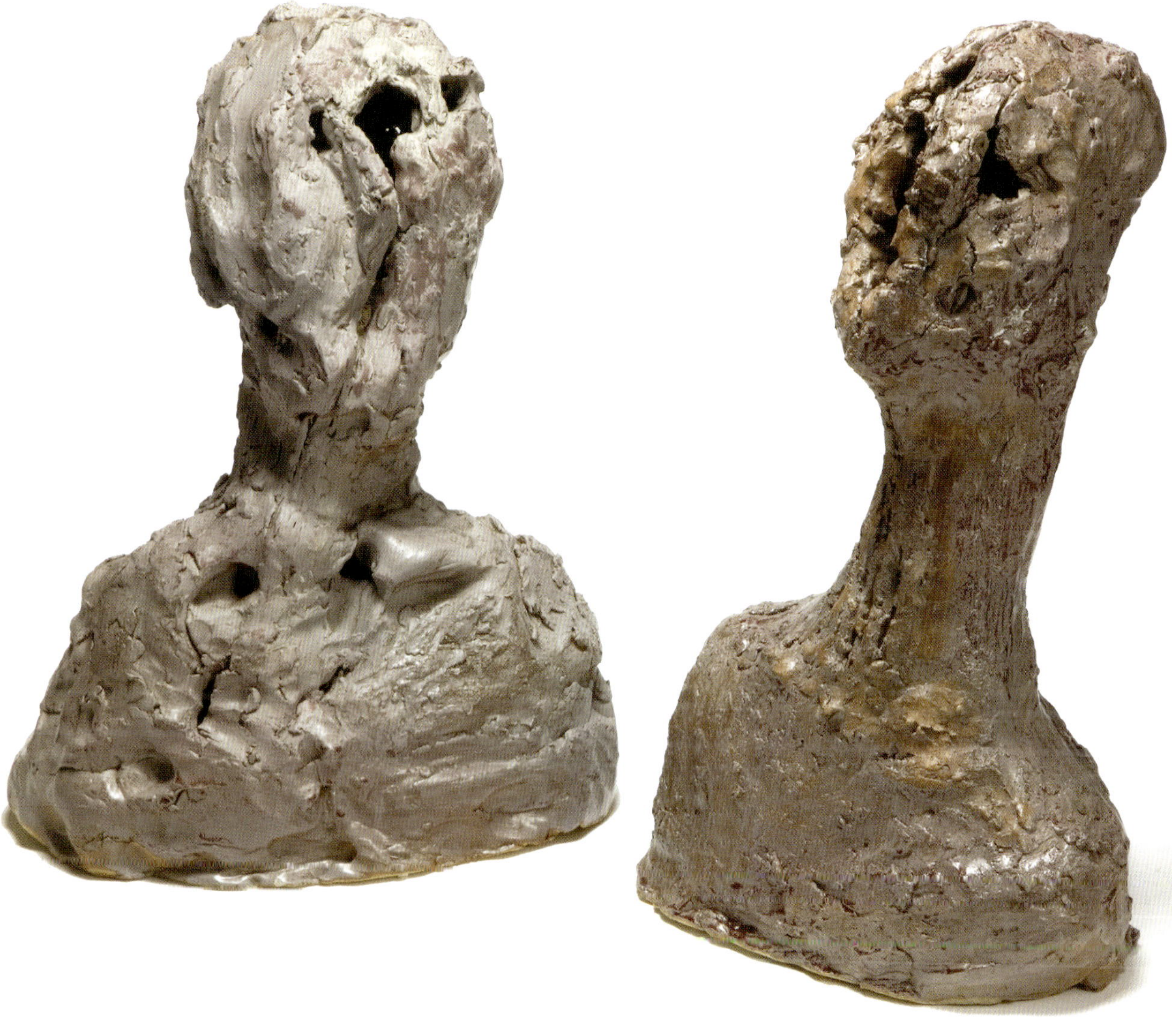

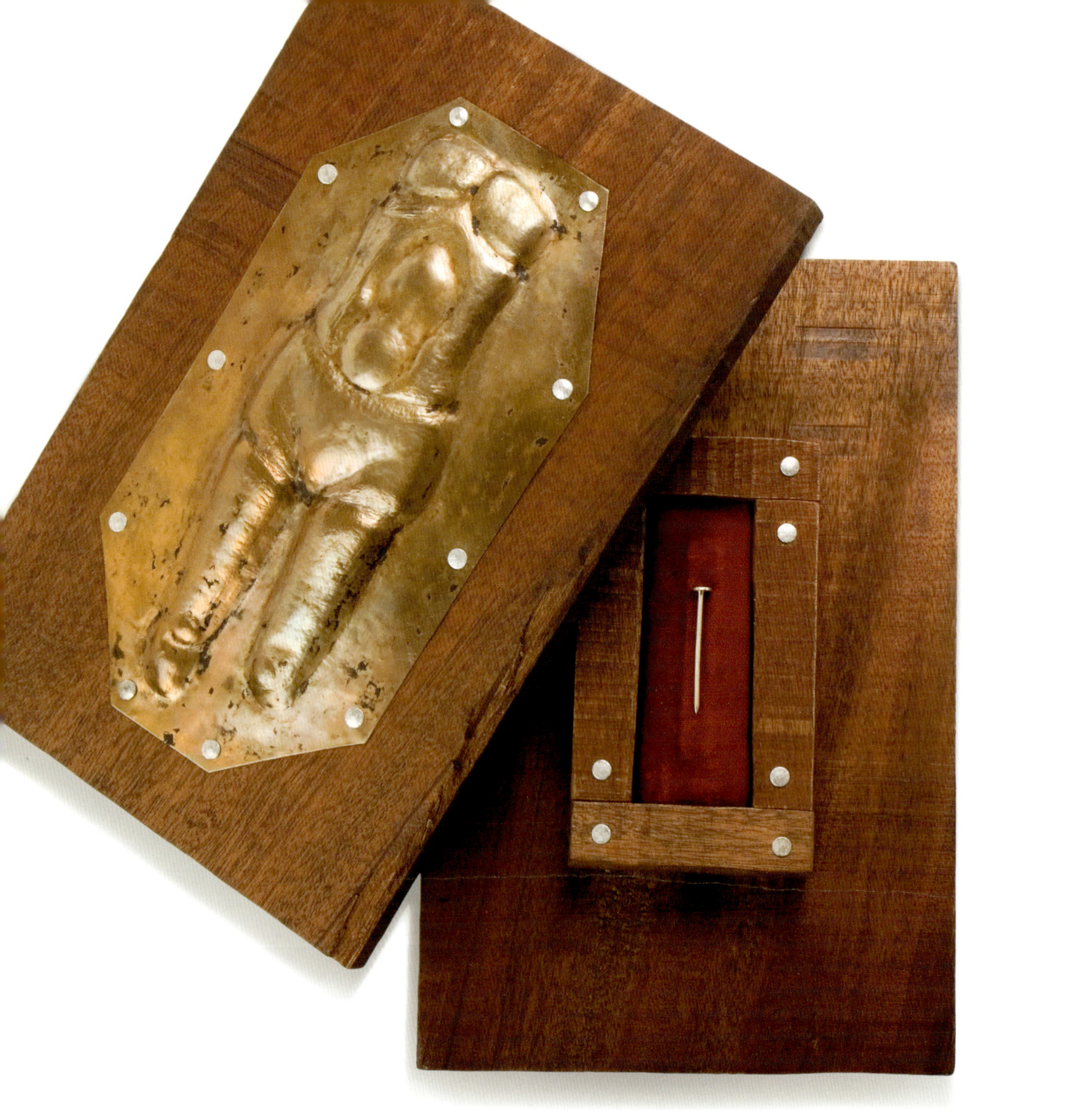

My chosen artifact was the fragmented, carved wooden body of Christ. I was inspired by its beautiful shape, form and detail. I felt as though I needed to incorporate or interpret its religious significance into my piece. The *Tesoros* exhibition influenced my understanding of what I wanted to create. I first decided to replicate the front of the body by chasing it in bronze, which later became the top of a mahogany box. When opened, a golden nail is exposed, enveloped by a bed of velvet. This is accompanied by a verse from The Bible, "Blessed are those who have not seen and yet have believed." John 20:29. When viewed within the context of my art, this has been the most challenging piece to create by far, and has made me question my reasons for making. It represents the discovery of a deeper concept and personal meaning that I have been striving for as an artist. This piece is a crucial addition to my body of work, and has helped me clarify the ideals and morals that I uphold and want to communicate through my art.

Taryn L. Backus

The Way, The Truth, and The Light (2007)

Gold
Silver
Bronze
Mahogany
Velvet
Olive Oil
14" x 9" x 3"

Melody L. Basch

Memento Mori (2006)

Copper
Sterling Silver
Stainless Steel
2″ x 1 1/4″ x 1/2″

The silver frame artifact must once have contained something precious. After the contents were lost, only the frame remained. Because it survived, the frame is now the object of importance.

The empty frame reminded me of an open mouth with teeth. It made me think about a human body decaying; all that is left are the bones and teeth, suggesting what has been lost. I made a brooch modeled on teeth from my family—those still living and those who have died.

What remains after we decay?

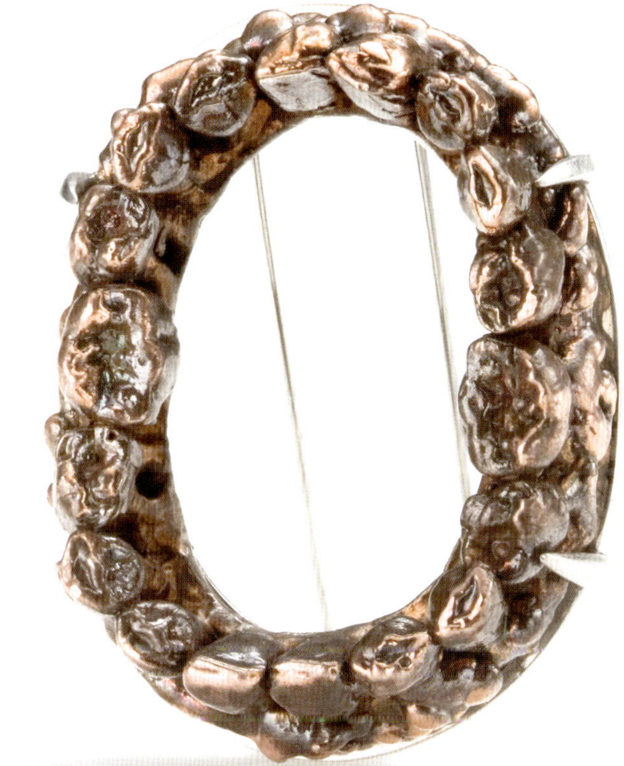

Marybeth E. Bent

Untitled (2007)

Black Delrin
Silver Wire
16" x 4" x ½" (necklace)
1¾" x 1½" x ½" (brooch)

Milagros are small charms that represent body parts and life's essentials. Worshippers pin them to the clothing of a statue of a saint in the hopes that their prayers will be answered. The sacred heart milagro can represent the heart of Jesus, a heart condition, or any matter of the heart. I was inspired to incorporate a heart shaped milagro into a carved plastic frame to be worn as a pendant. In the process of making, I struggled to balance the delicate and precious nature of the milagro with the weight and scale of the plastic. Ultimately I decided to make two pieces, one being a large heart form, and the other a small brooch enshrining the milagro. They are to be worn together, a form of prayer, depending on what you believe.

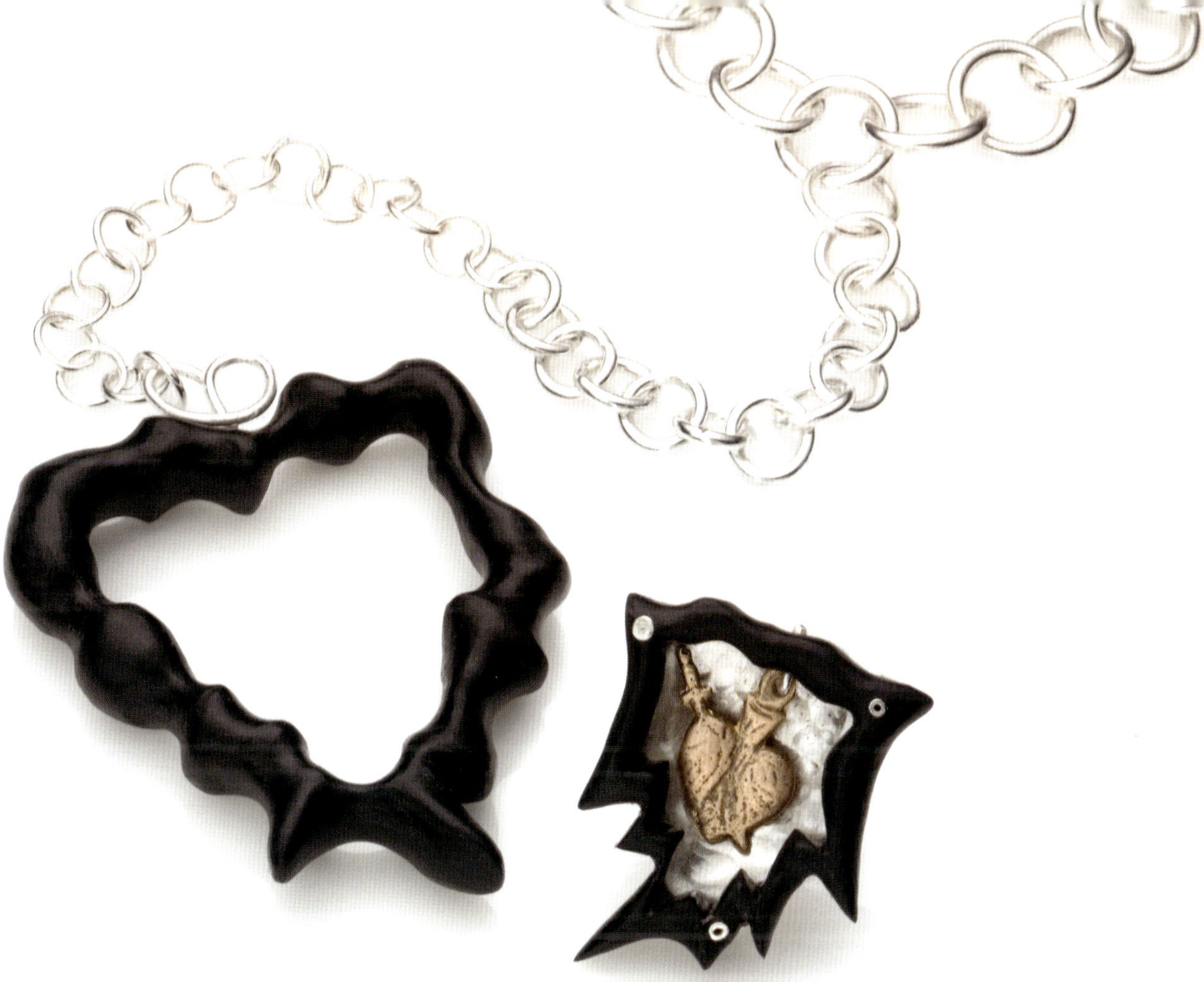

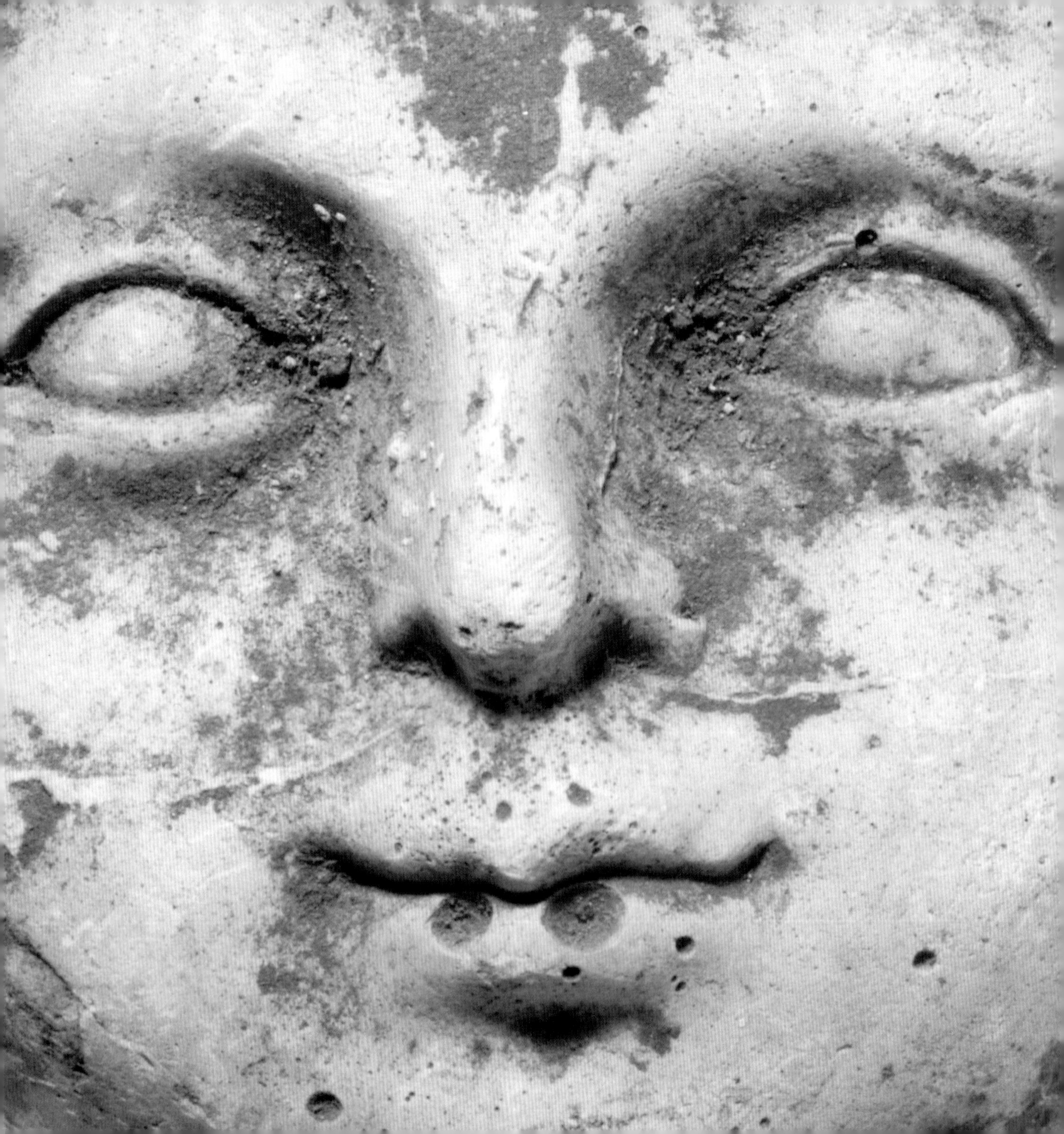

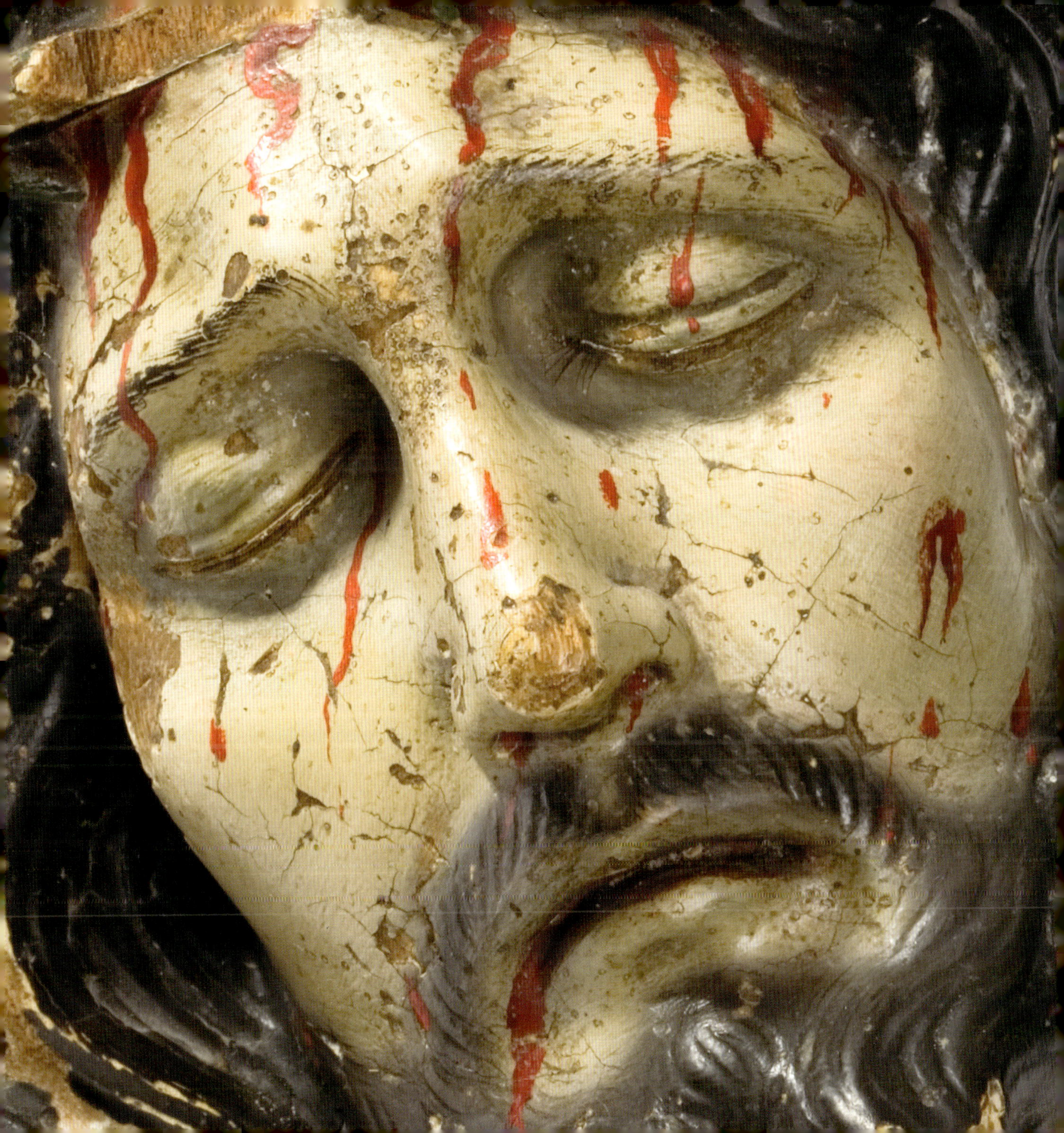

Sarah A. Bernard

Maravella (2007)

14K Red Gold
Sterling Silver
Plaster Bust (Artifact)
10″ x 10″ x 4″

I was immediately drawn to this small plaster bust of a woman for her beauty and simplicity. Her anonymity made me wonder about who she might have been. I wanted to give her a character that would enhance her elegance and sophistication. I also wanted to give her a life and personality. Knowing she was a colonial Mexican artifact, I honored her culture by using a marigold, the traditional Day of the Dead altar flower, to adorn her. I also made a necklace to surround her, frame her, and add to her natural beauty.

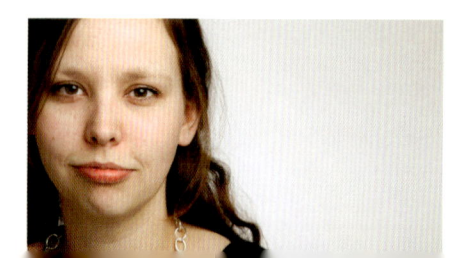

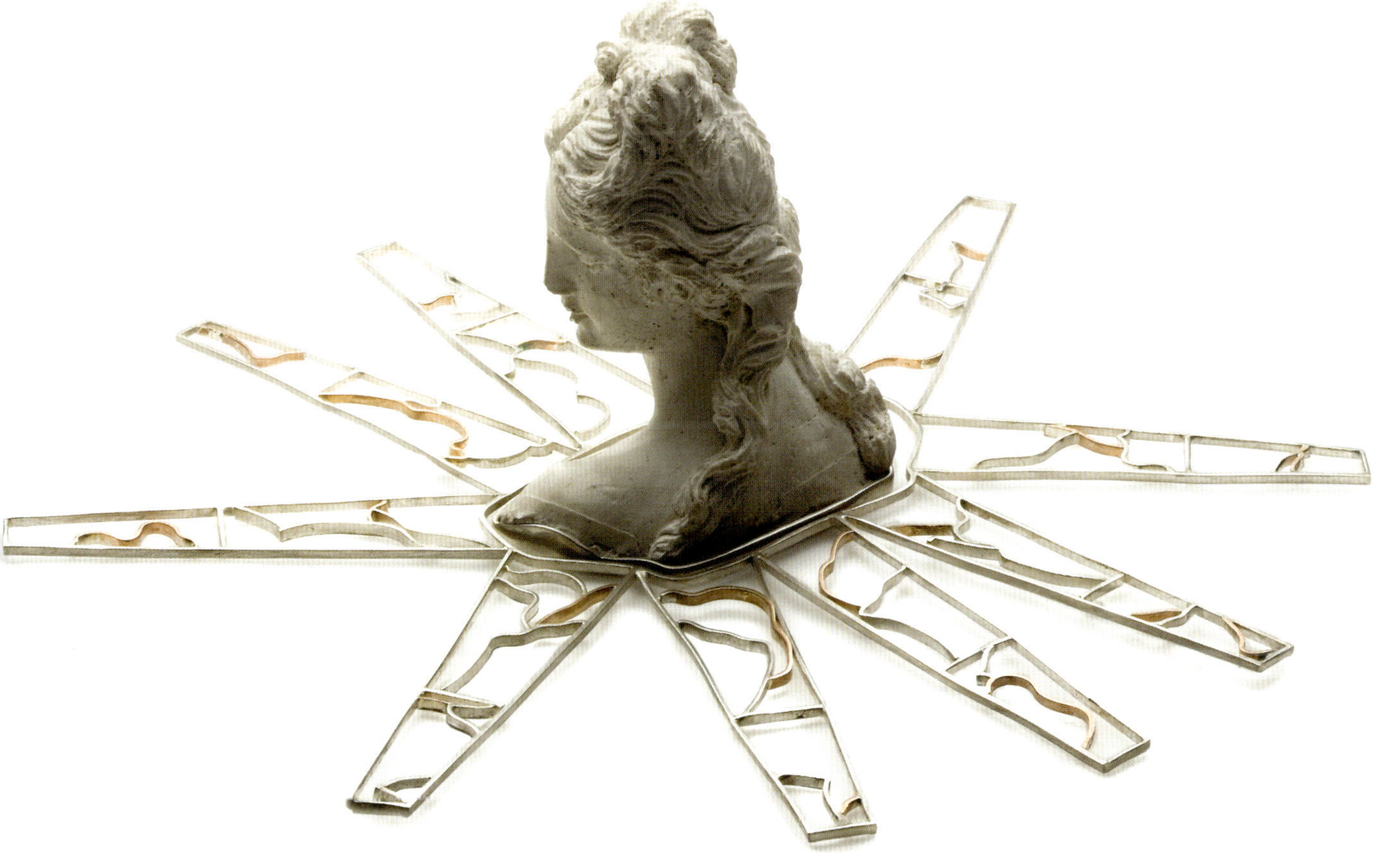

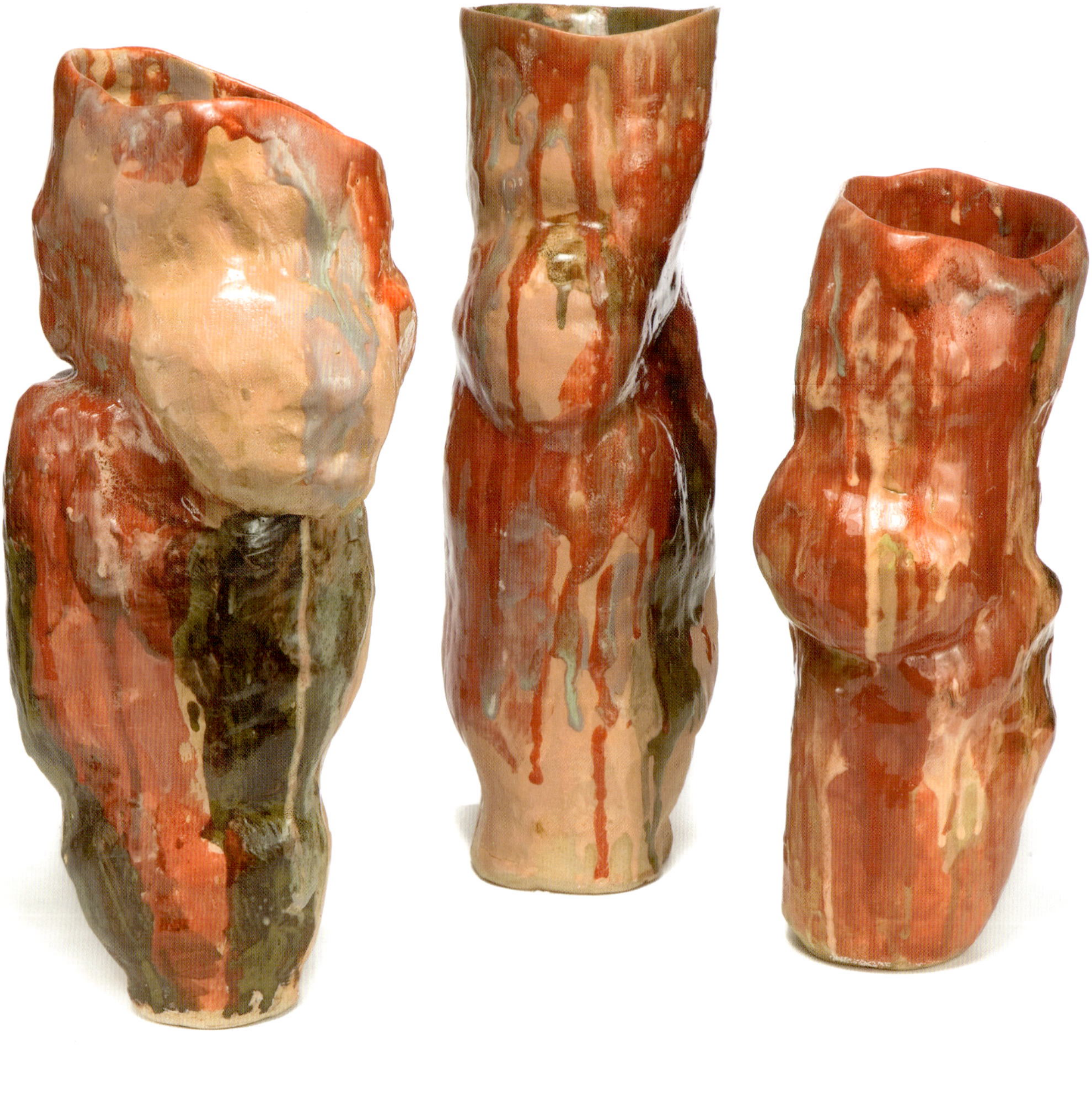

The painted wooden figure of Christ was inspiration for my piece. The artifact instantly appealed to me. Wood is not a medium I work in but I am extremely drawn to the aesthetic and narrative value of woodcarving. Through this project I experimented with carving bone-dry clay as if it were wood. The visual results are very similar. The *Tesoros* exhibit was also inspiration for my work, primarily through color. While the deep, rich color choices of the artists of that time and culture make their work look refined and royal, this dramatic effect also presents images of blood and sacrifice, an effect which I used in my work for this project.

Emily R. Bixler

Legs (2007)

Stoneware
15 ¾" x 4 ¼" (1)
16 ½" x 5 ½" (2)
13" x 4 ½" (3)

Chase M. Brown

Crown of Thorns (2007)

Stoneware
48″ x 16″ x 16″

The piece that I have created is inspired by the Jesus Christ head. More specifically, it is inspired by the crown of thorns that Jesus wore. I have always admired much Christian art for its expressiveness and depth, but had never found any personal connection to it. Not being a religious person, I view religion from an outsider's perspective. With that said, I had to ask myself what the crown of thorns represents to others, since it has never held any significance for me. I was drawn to the crown of thorns due to the organic form of the thorns and branches. I have always been inspired by nature and the connection seemed obvious to me. I chose to construct my *Misterios* project using juxtaposed thrown forms that create the crown of thorns. I left the surface of the clay rough with the throwing marks evident, which gives an organic feel to the surface. The crown of thorns symbolizes pain and suffering. I wanted my piece to look as though it would be painful to wear upon your head.

While making this project I learned a lot about myself and what inspires me. I also learned a lot about gravity and how to defy it. Searching for inspiration is difficult when it is in something that you do not believe in or does not interest you very much. I used the crown of thorns as a connection to my own work because I was inspired by its organic form. It took me a while to find that connection. But once it had been established, my outlook on the *Misterios* project changed, and I became very motivated.

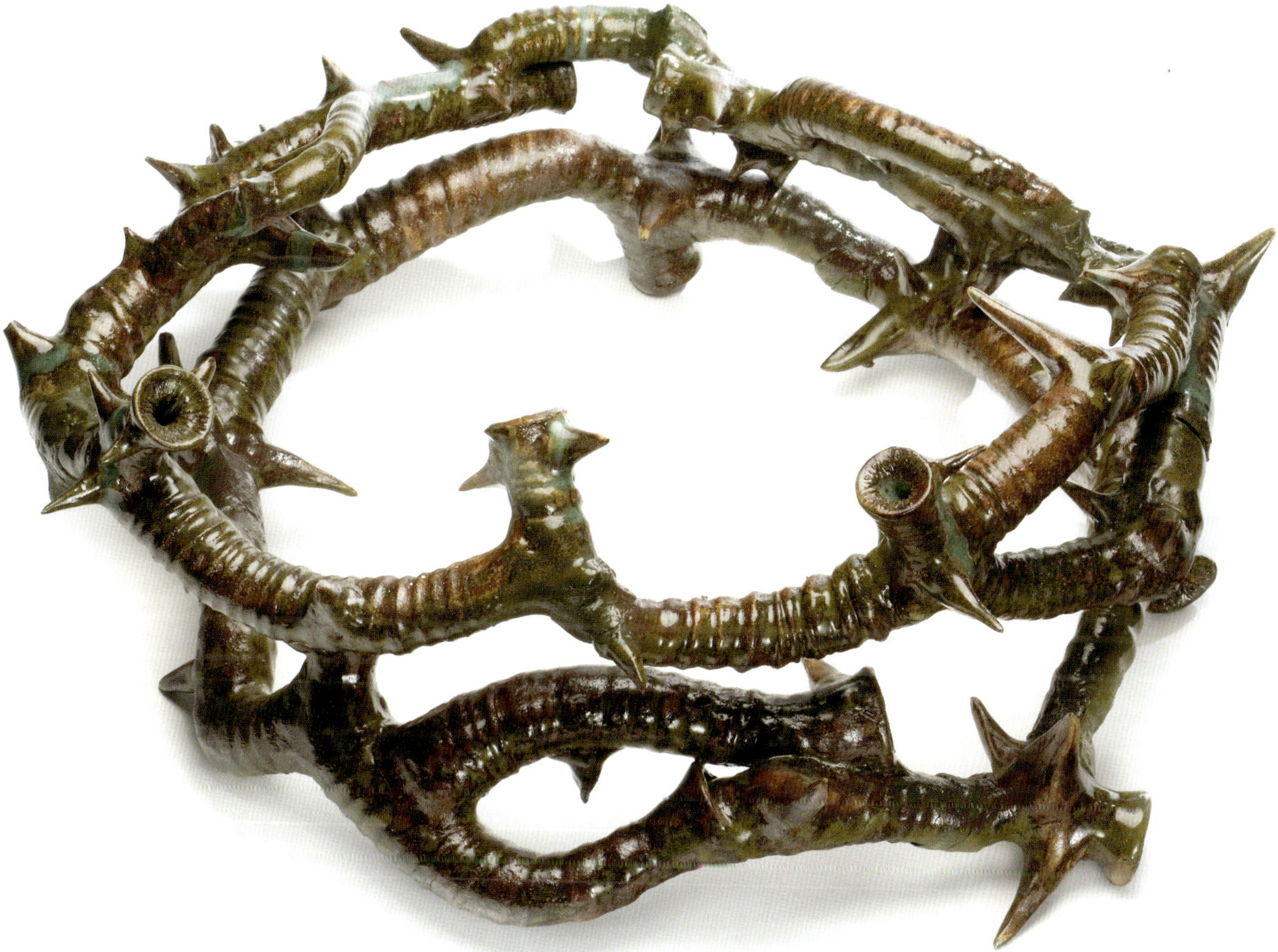

044 MISTERIOS

The Mexican culture celebrates life in a colorful and beautiful way on the Day of the Dead. This inspired me to create a narrative of that type of celebration in the form of a necklace. I chose to use a resin cherub head printed on the 3-D computer-modeling printer, which was a replica of an actual artifact. I thought of the many ways families have to accept death through tears, flowers and mourning, comforted by the knowledge that they are delivering a loved one into the hands of God. I frequently watch *Miami Ink,* a television show that follows life in a tattoo parlor, so I thought of tattoos that people get in memory of loved ones and their need to put these images on their bodies, close to their hearts.

With this in mind, I made a necklace of hands, flowers, and tears to wear near the heart.

Nina R. Brown

In God's Hands (2007)

Sterling Silver
Copper
Bronze
Resin
15" x 6" x 1 ½"

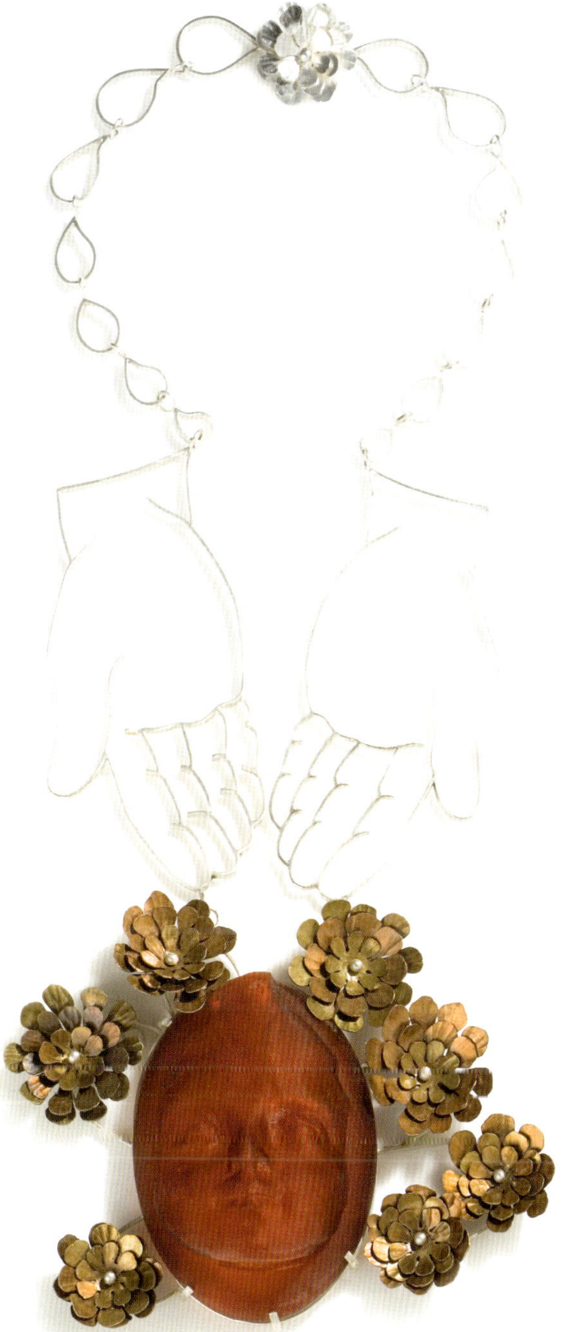

Chun Chun

Monkey and Child (2007)

Bronze
Sterling Silver
4″ x 3″

When I first saw the miniature plaster bust of a woman in classical Greek Style, I knew she must be a goddess. I wanted to work in that style, and started immediately, but the image I first created was not perfect enough for me. I felt so upset and lost; I gave myself a break and looked at my previous artwork. Most of my work is joyous, humorous and cartoon-like. I realized that I needed to make my own funky goddess—a monkey—with her child.

I was so happy to find my passion within this project. I have learned to bring that to all of my artwork.

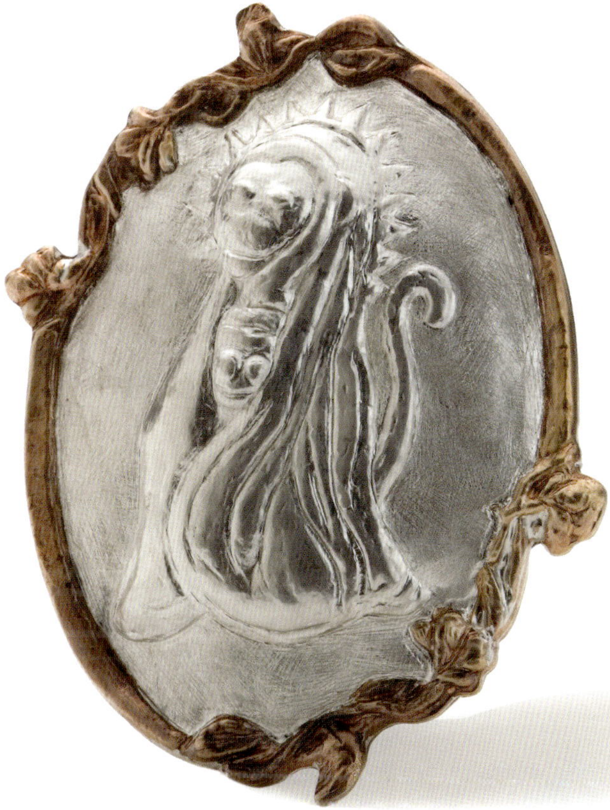

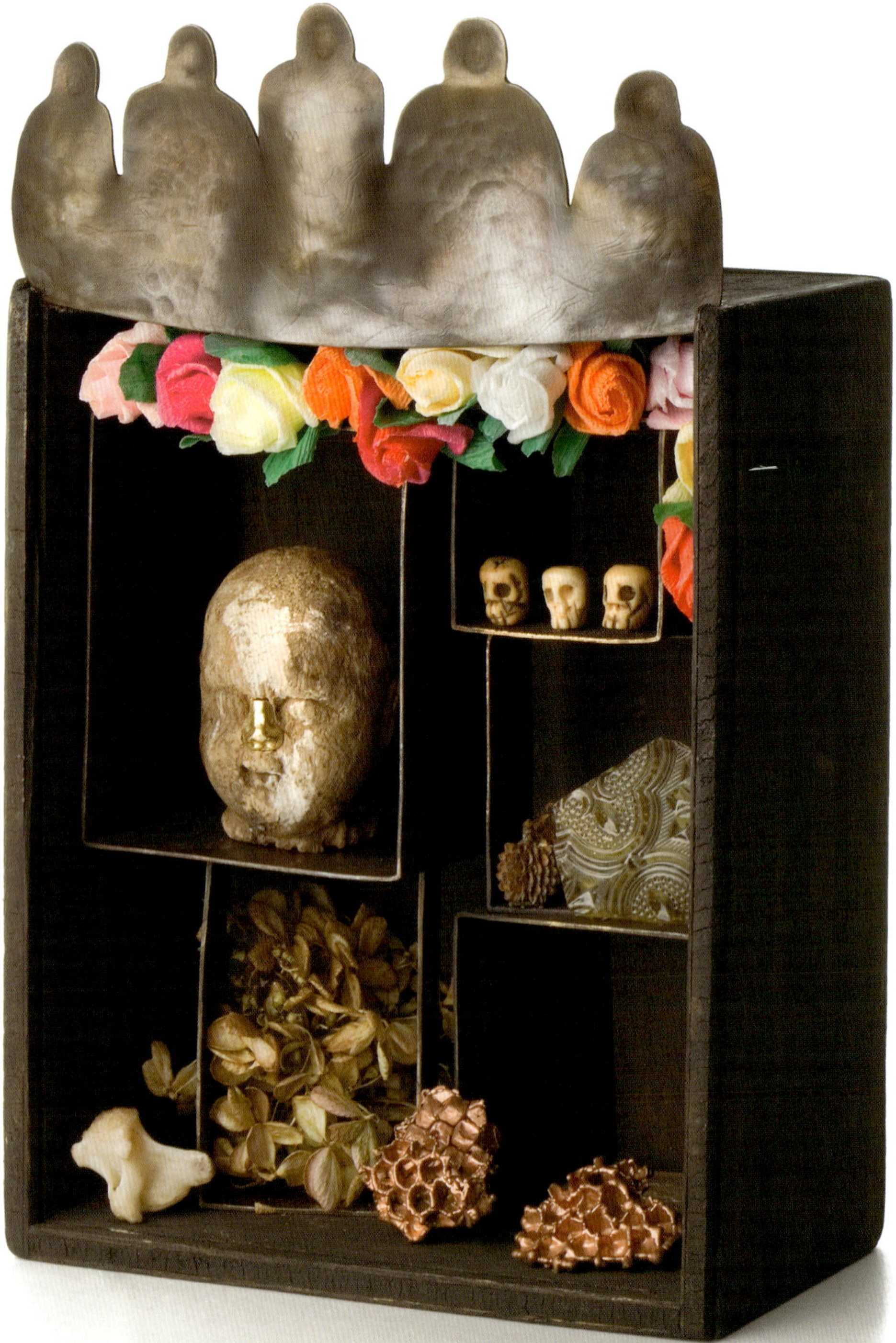

I chose to make a memento mori, cenotaph for the wooden baby head artifact. The nose on this small wood head was missing, so I made a gold nose for it. Because I spent my formative years in Mexico, the objects that are contained in this piece mirror that culture.

My intention is to have the imagery in this piece reflect the transience of life.

Marianne E. Contreras

En Esta Vida Todo Se Paga (2006)

Mixed Media
5 ⅛" x 9" x 3 ¼"

050 MISTERIOS

The artifact I chose to interpret is the series of milagros. Milagros, meaning miracles, are Latin American charms that are used as prayer offerings. For example, if one is about to undergo a heart operation, one might pin a milagro in the shape of a heart to an altar and pray for a successful surgery.

I chose to create my own series of milagros based on our society's most common request for health and wellness. Each milagro I created represents a different body ailment or illness. Keeping with my previous work that often deals with nostalgic imagery, I used Shrinky Dinks to create drawings of each ailment, similar to images found in children's anatomy textbooks. I crafted a milagro with a feeling of warmth and protection by crocheting wool frames around each image as a way to protect and comfort each prayer on its way to becoming a "miracle."

Christine Domanic

Milagros (2007)

Wool
Cotton
Shrink Film
26" x 20"

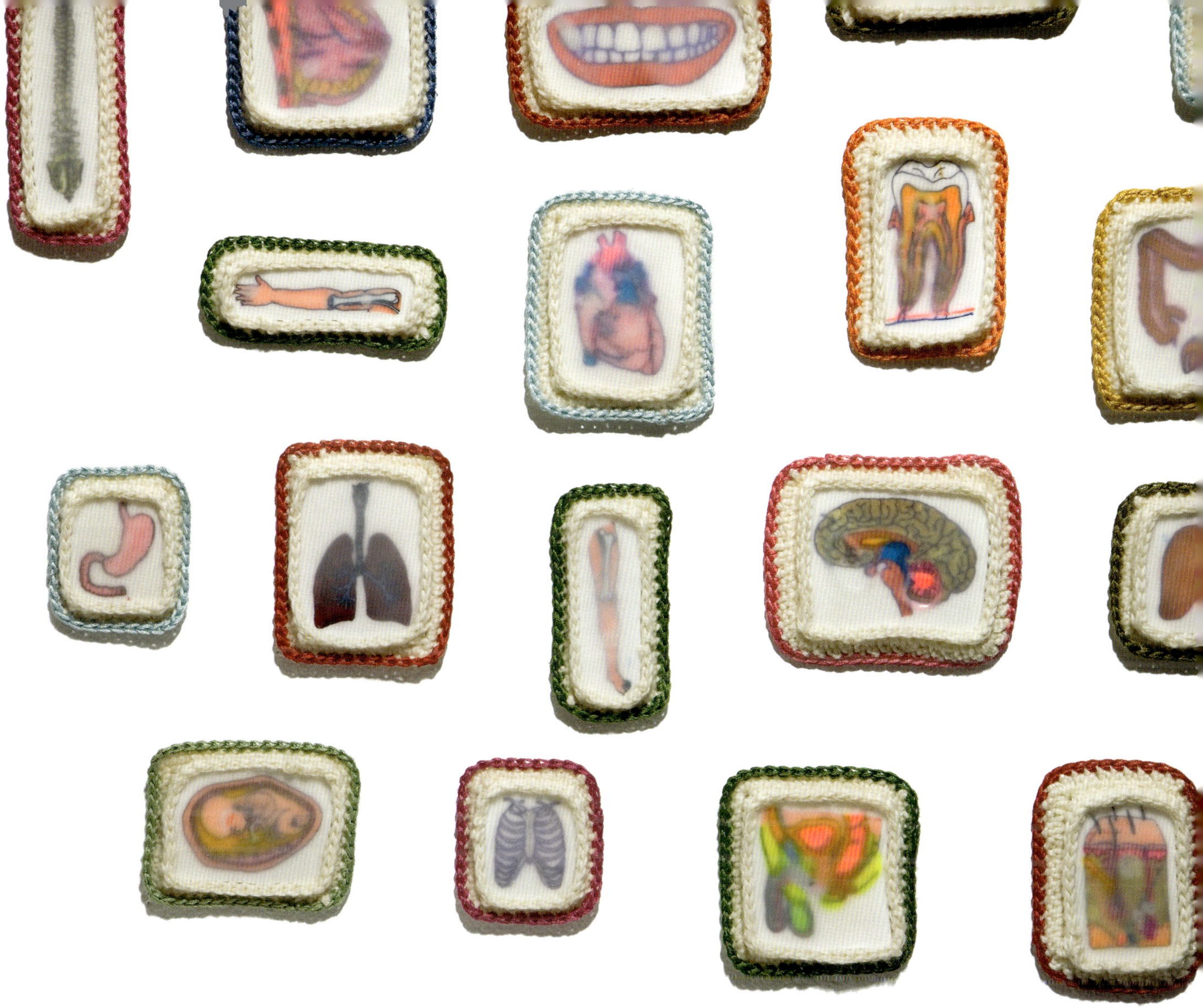

MISTERIOS

The painted icon of Christ inspired me because I understand and admire the need for human beings to make a representation of who or what they believe in. Paint has chipped off of the traditional sheet metal "canvas," removing much of the image of Christ. I was happy with the artifact's deterioration, preferring it over a flawless entirety.

I have created my own devotional image of someone very dear to me—my guardian angel, whom I have known and loved since adolescence. Using the same materials of icon painters in Mexico, I crafted his image until I thought it was complete.

Initially, my painting was bright, clean and carefully worked. Yet, it wasn't until the image became purposefully obscured that I realized it was more alive. Candles, melted drop by drop, flow over the image like tears, creating a multi-layered veil of emotion. This meditative technique is similar to processes used throughout my work. The holy figure has become a mystery—elusive and sealed with my adoration.

Desiree D. Fabela

Cherubim Mekin (2007)

Wood
Tin
Pewter
Oils
Wax
16" x 15" x 6"

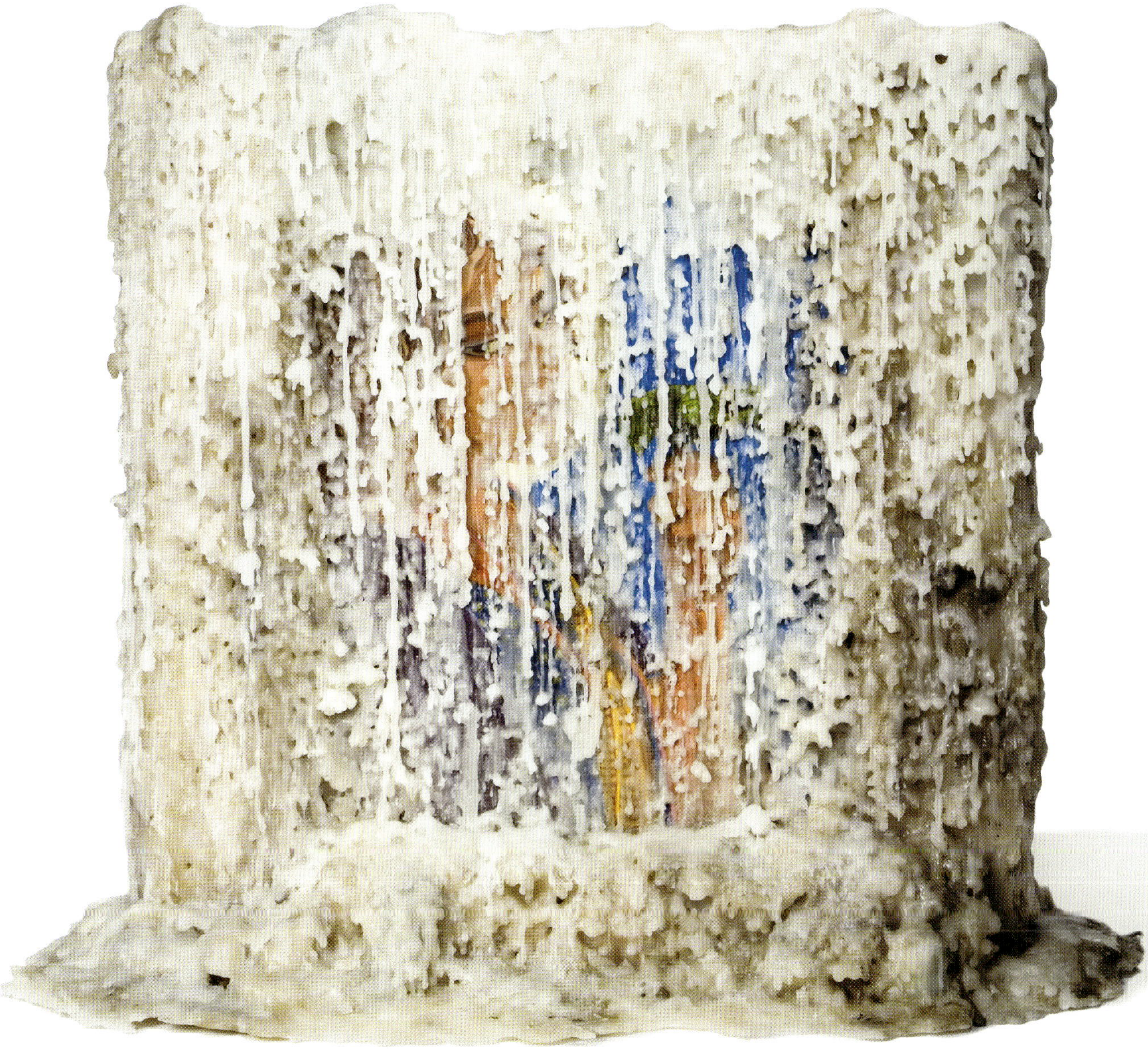

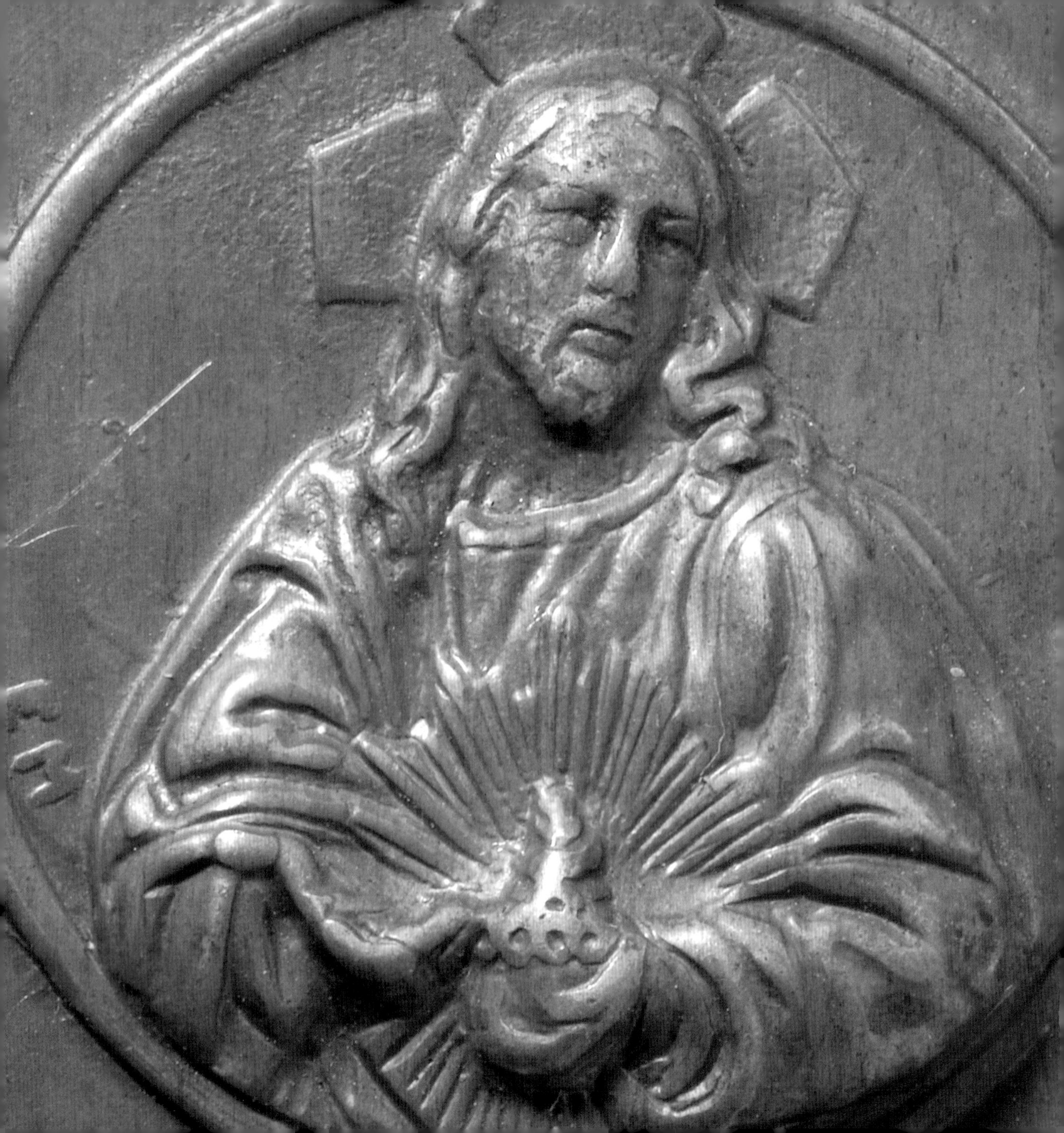

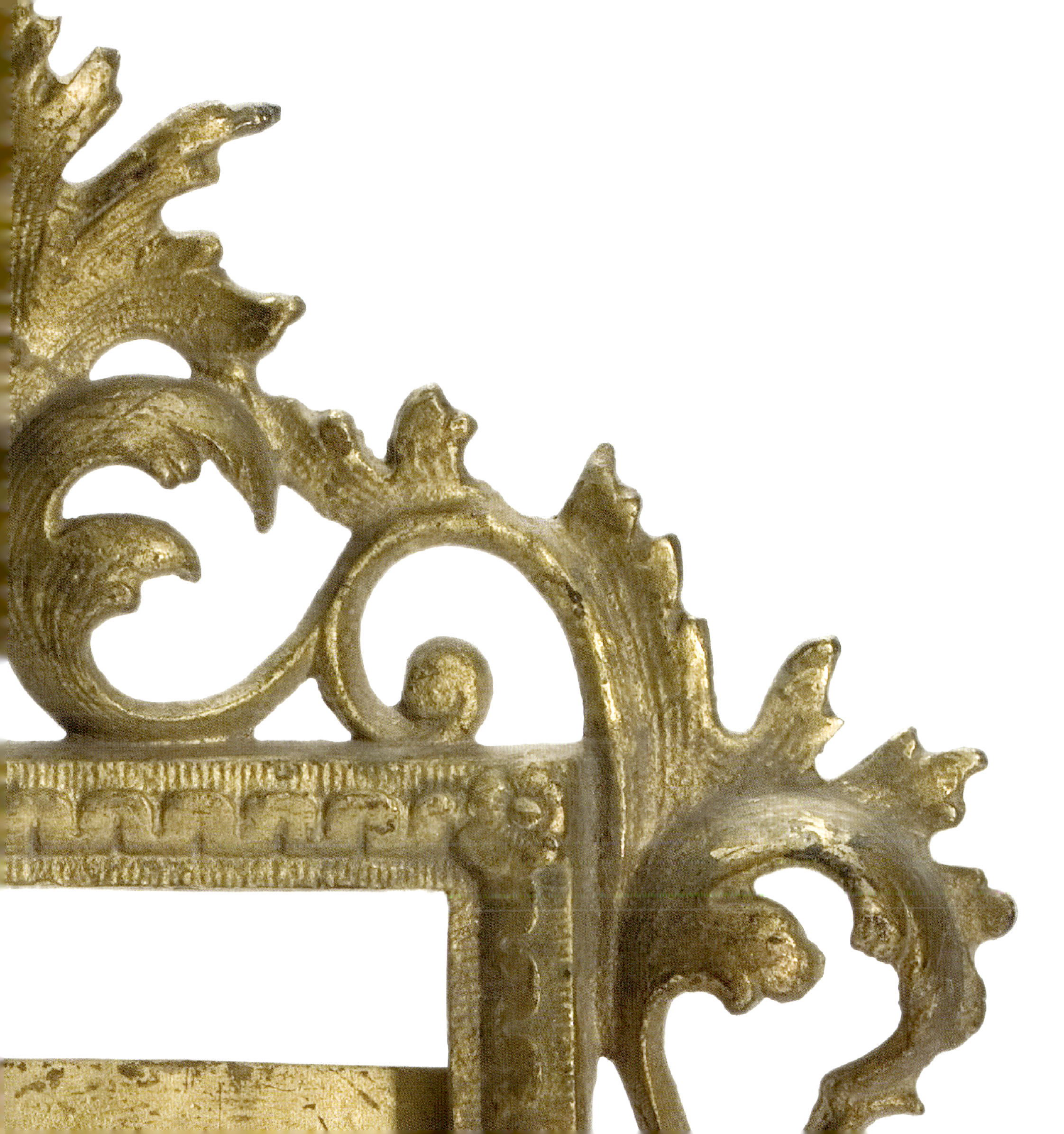

William R. Fetzer

This Is A Frame (2007)

Stoneware
24″ x 10″

The rather small bronze frame with Baroque designs sticking out on all four sides became inspiration for my piece. I was immediately drawn to the frame because, knowing the way I work, I could be the most creative with this particular artifact. In order to make the forms I envisioned, I had to use a machine for clay called an extruder. Using the extruder allowed me to create perfectly round hollow tubes for the top of my piece, and this experience became the most exciting aspect of this project. It is something that I am grateful to have learned how to do and it has led me to design some wonderful pieces that I am excited to begin. I feel that this experience has helped me grow as an artist, in that I learned a new process and worked my hardest to perfect it.

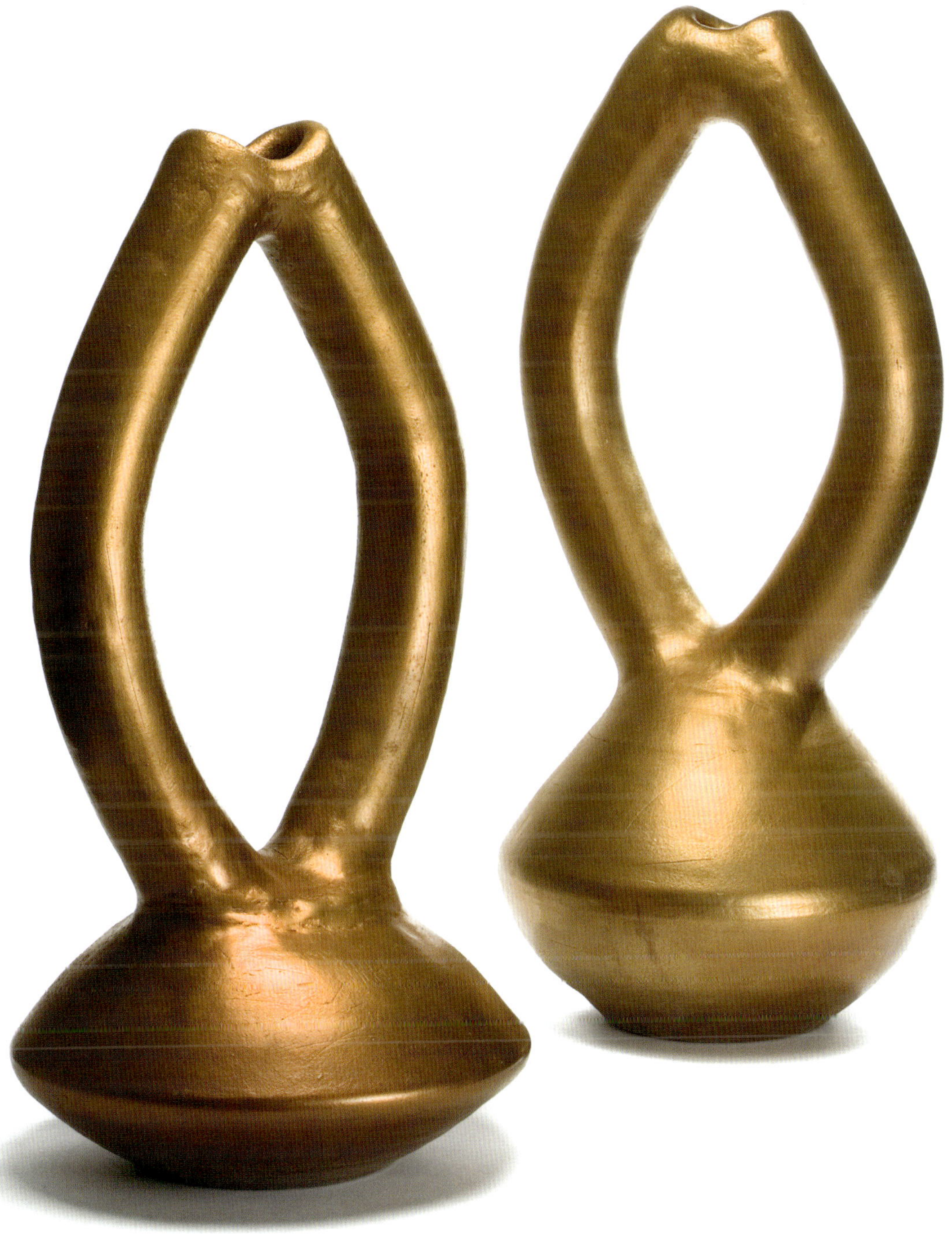

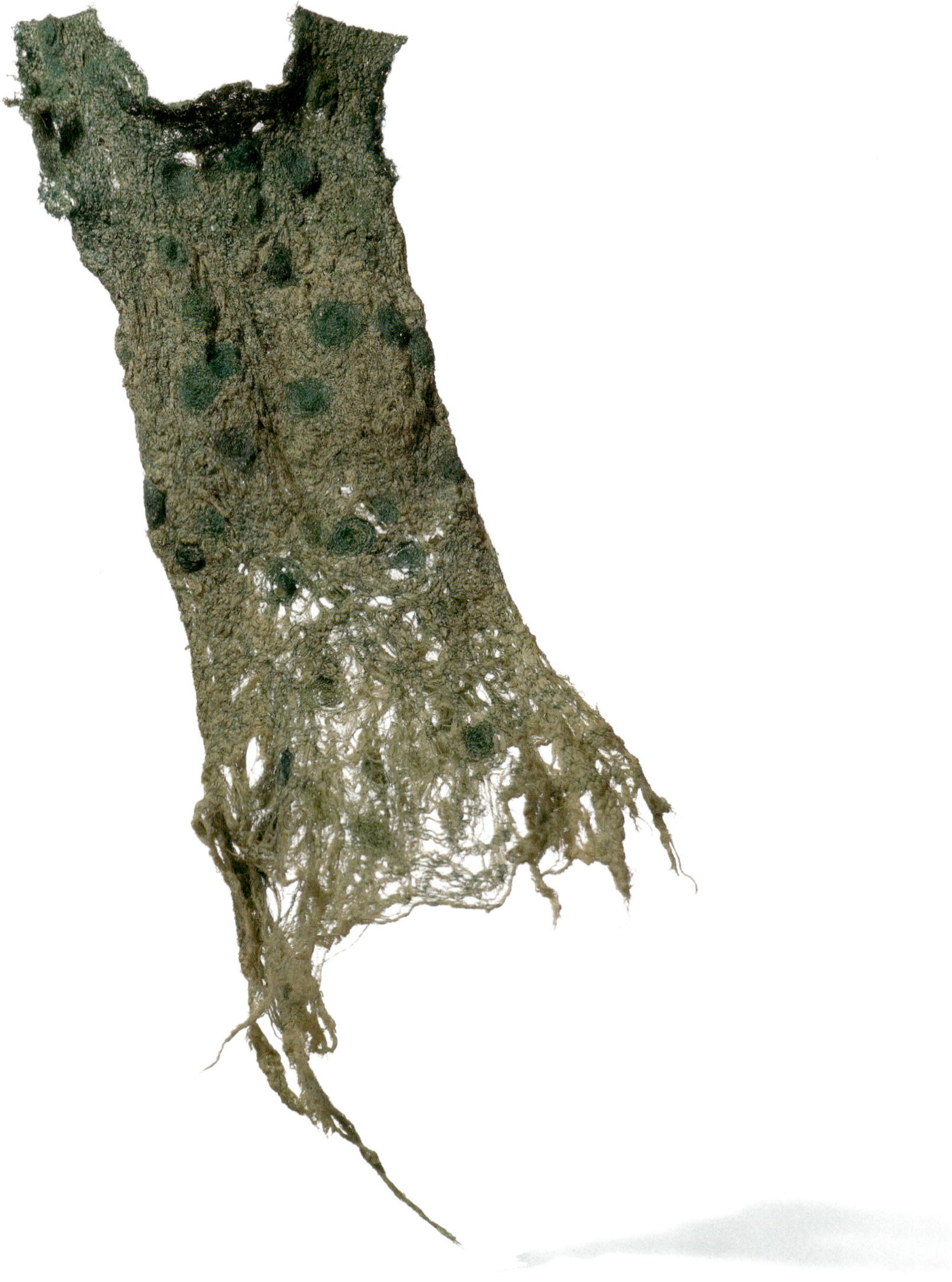

Milagros are small pins people tacked onto robes of saints as a hope and a symbol of healing. My piece was inspired by these ideas of healing. I made a garment out of embroidery that depicts cells regenerating, creating a "skin," something new and sturdy. The piece as a whole represents the process of creating or repairing something, and the emotions that come with it. The bottom of my garment is torn. It looks depressing, as if hurt. As the eye travels upward, it gradually becomes whole, calming, and healthy.

The piece relates to my other work in the sense that I am always thinking about growth—whether physical, emotional or figurative. I might even reference lack of growth. I strive to transform my average materials into a material that looks and feels different and carries its meaning or significance successfully.

Amanda J. Foss

Untitled (2007)

Gauze
Sewing Thread
36" x 15"

During my visit to the *Tesoros* exhibit, I was struck by the simultaneous feelings of attraction and revulsion I had for the works I saw. Having worked on religious iconography in the past, I felt a familiar struggle between the idea of creating a precious image as a pure offering to a higher power, and the hypocrisy of using treasured materials, such as gold and jewels, which turn a sacred image into a material object to be lusted after. My past work in fibers has involved weaving, sewing and needlework, and in order to translate my ideas about iconography and materialism, I used this very intensive version of embroidery and embellishment. I was given a silver frame and designed this piece to fit inside the artifact. I created my version of a modern icon to express my feelings about the materialization of our culture by representing a corporate logo, Paris Hilton, as my Virgin Mary and adorning her with couture and jewels.

Katharine M. Fraser

Our Lady Paris (2007)

Thread
Glass Beads
Brass Pins
Colonial Mexican Silver Frame (Artifact)
5" x 4"

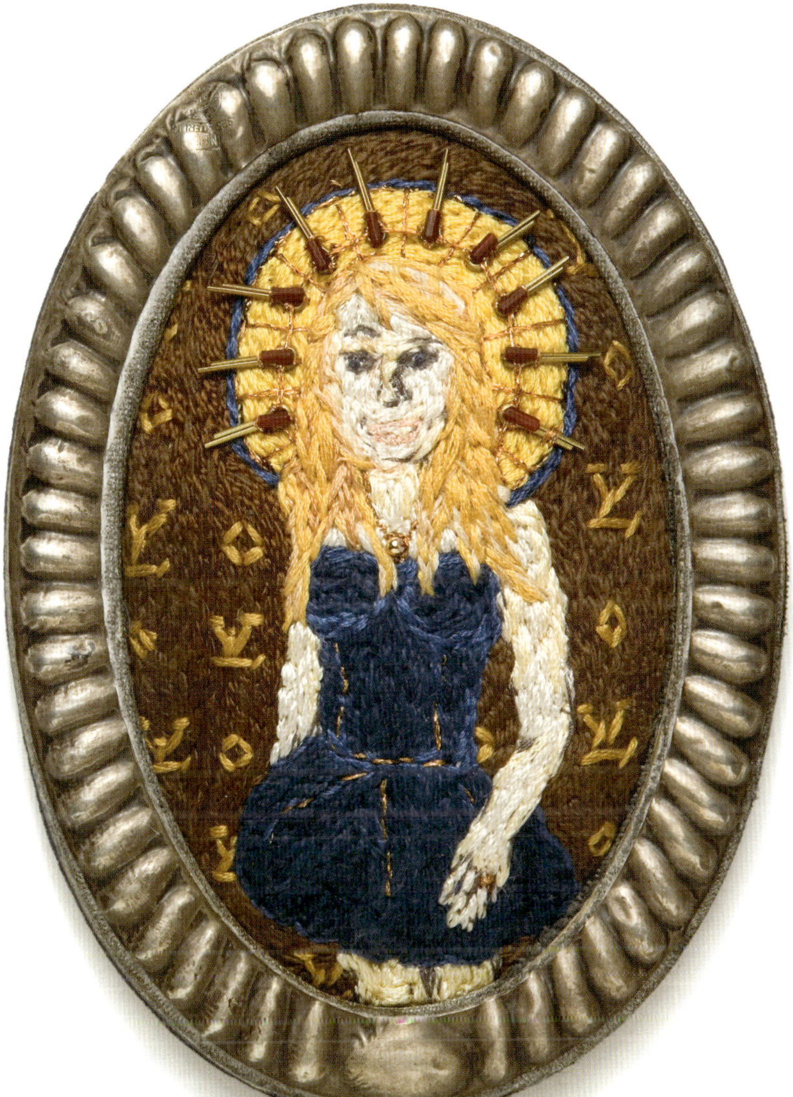

For this assignment, I chose to respond to the armless, headless polychrome wooden sculpture of Christ. I was immediately captivated by the pose of the figure in its fragmented form and was intrigued by its dead, gray tones and macabre implications. This assignment invited me to study many facets of Mayan, pre-Hispanic and Colonial American arts and culture. I was particularly intrigued by the ornate surfaces on Mayan architectural facades, with designs featuring geometric, bodily references. I also explored the notion of a culture facing pressures of revolution and change, and empathized with the men and women whose existence on earth is exhausted by spiritual suffocation. Through coiling — a traditional basketry technique — I've built a torso form which begins to mimic the artifact, yet seems to float somewhere between solidity and fragility. The form is hollow, indicating the capacity for a human body, yet it is inevitably empty. My hope is that this piece exists somewhere between form and function, armor and armature, sculpture and craft.

With regard to my own work, past and future, this experience allowed me to expand on what I have discovered from coiling in a sculptural context. I generally choose to work figuratively; in the past this has manifested itself in real or imagined biological organs and organisms. In this piece, I'm beginning to deal with the body more as structure or architecture.

Megan S. Frisch

Untitled (2006)

Electrical Wire
Thread
Acrylic Gel
16" x 10" x 27"

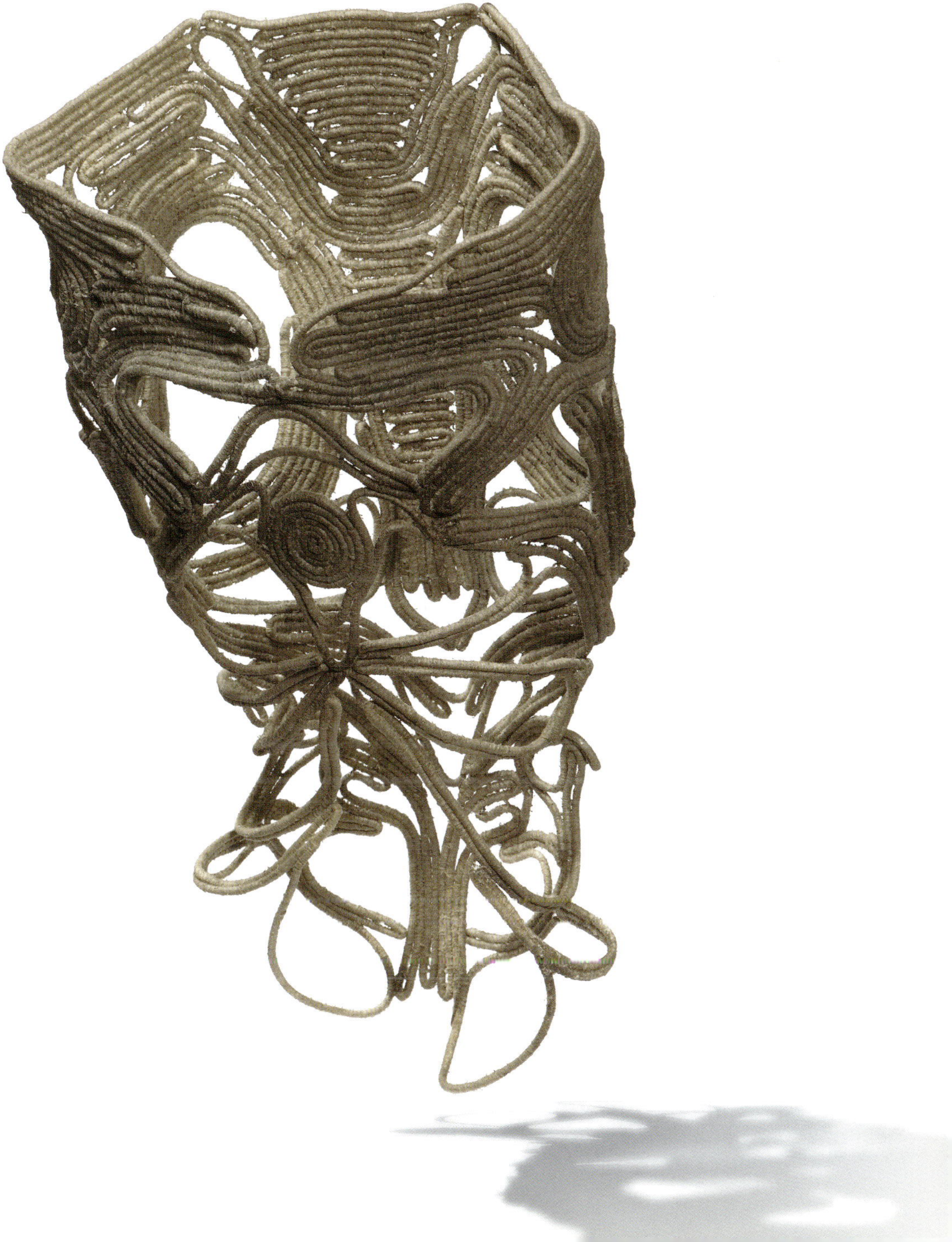

"I plunder you, I crush you, I kill you, but I save you."

"Te saqueo, te aplasto, te mato, pero te salvo." This comment is attributed to an unnamed French writer during the time of the European influx, speaking of the influence of Christianity in the new world (translated into Spanish).

I was given the icon of Jesus, a small painting on metal, which I incorporated into my piece. I'd done some informal research concerning the clash of the indigenous cultures of the Americas with that of the Spanish settlers. One book in particular that influenced this work is called "American Holocaust," an unsentimental and unsparingly detailed account of the near annihilation of the Native Americans by the Europeans. I had also read a brief newspaper article about the discovery of a new species of bird in an Andean "cloud forest"— a term I'd never heard before—and this information influenced the physical form my work would take. The bird was named the "Yariguies brush finch" to memorialize the tribe of people that had once lived in the area before the arrival of the Spanish. Apparently the Yariguies had committed mass suicide rather than submit to the Spanish.

I thought it fitting to build a mountaintop shrouded in clouds, a reference to the natural world the Yariguies inhabited. It's a landscape that in part still remains. Rather than emphasize the icon, I chose to inter it beneath the mountain, out of view. This work is a tribute to animism/ mysticism, but is also an indictment of destruction that masquerades as salvation.

Sara C. Gallo

Mountain with Jesus Sculpture (2007)

Ceramic
14 ½" x 15 ¼" x 19"

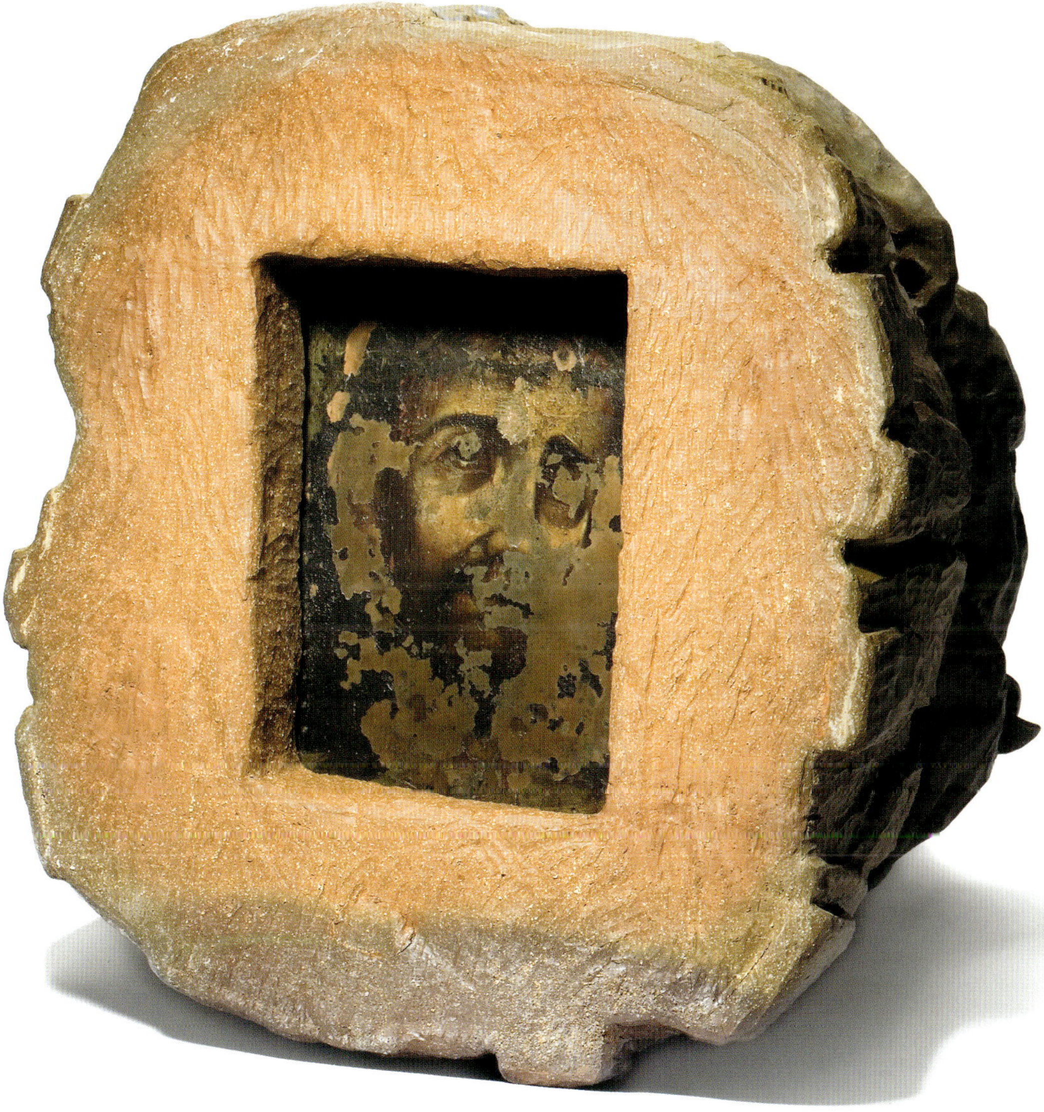

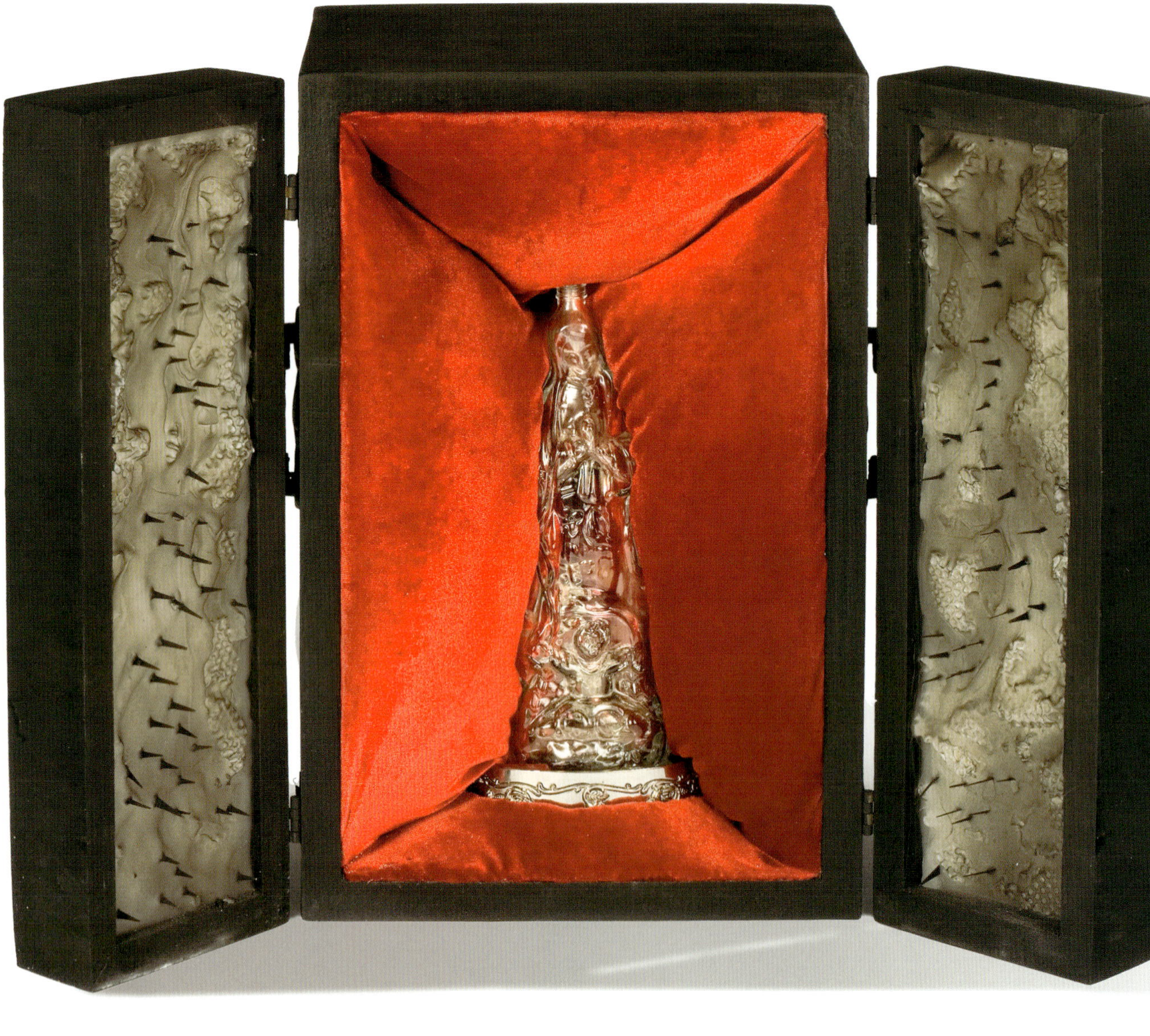

Jennifer M. Gin

Nesting Place (2006)

Glass Bottle
Straws
Wax
Wood
Found Objects
15" x 10" x 10"

I chose the glass bottle of the Virgin Mary as my artifact because I was drawn to its familiarity and preciousness. After experiencing the religious nature of the *Tesoros* exhibition at the Philadelphia Museum of Art, I wanted to create a shrine as well as a dwelling for the bottle. The most important aspect of the piece is to maintain anonymity with its exterior in order to highlight the precious quality of the bottle through the interior.

068   MISTERIOS

Latin American art and culture finds exquisite beauty in pain and suffering—even death. I incorporated this concept into my work by transforming a painful personal experience into a precious object. On one side of the pendant is an image related to my previous work, where I manipulated my own body and photographed it in such a way that the image was ambiguous, possessing qualities that became beautiful in their grotesqueness. On the other side of the pendant hangs the artifact I worked with, a tiny charm referred to as a milagro. It was chosen for its literal imagery of a little girl and its symbolic meaning of hope and redemption.

Genava L. Gisondi

A Proper Burial (2007)

Patinated Sterling Silver
23K Gold
Ruby
Shredded & Burned Silk
36″ x 8″ (Necklace as a whole)
4″ x 2″ (Pendant only)

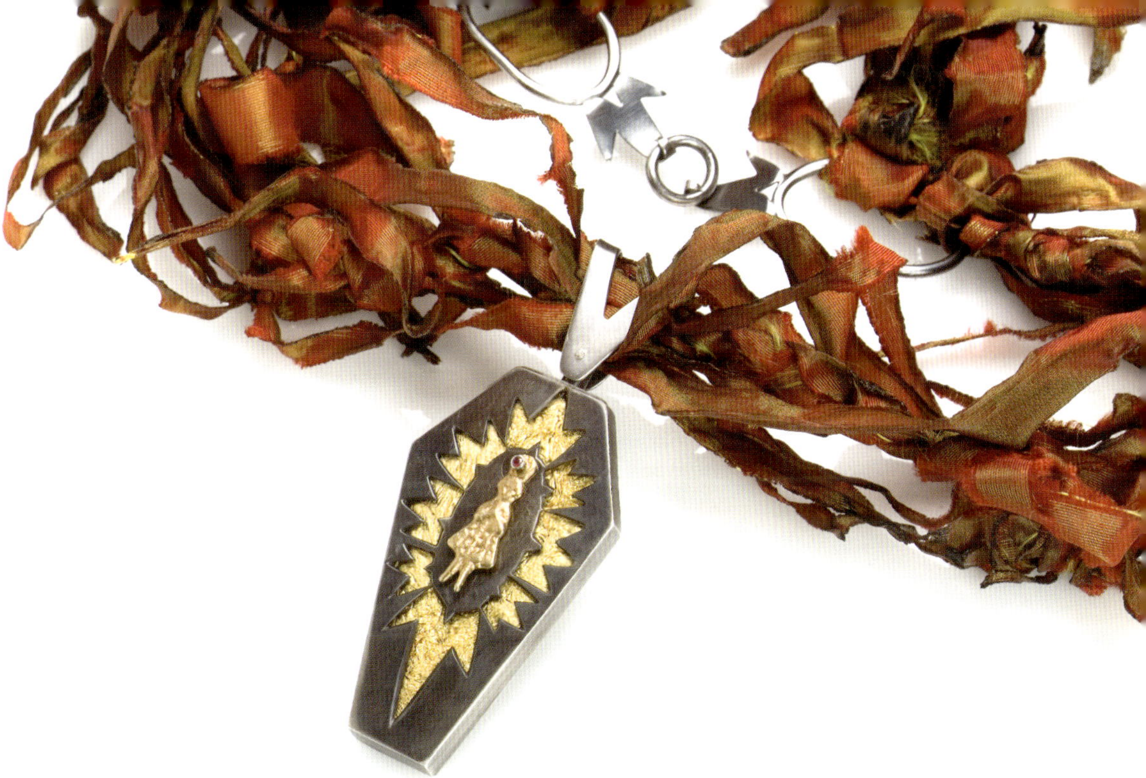

Religion has always played an integral part in my life; I am not very religious but it helps to put my purpose on earth into perspective. I was raised Jewish and most of what I know about religion I learned in Hebrew school. I have been lucky enough to travel to Europe a few times and have been exposed to tons of Catholic churches and art. The image in Catholicism that intrigues me most, yet horrifies me, is the image of Christ on the crucifix. I always saw the power in it but I never understood the idea of using fear to enforce belief. I chose my object because it is not the typical representation of a bleeding Christ. Instead, it is a more welcoming object, rather than one that intends to invoke fear.

I decided to build a small chest of drawers inspired by the numerous writing desks in the *Tesoros* exhibition; one in particular had an altar piece in the top center. I wanted to make my own version for sacred objects, not necessarily for writing utensils. My design consists of fourteen 5″ x 5″ drawer boxes with the plaster face of Jesus in its own glass "cubicle." The drawers do not have pulls because they are meant to hold sacred objects that should only be accessed on specific occasions. When the occasion arises the user takes the cubicle out of its spot and places its back to the drawer that needs to be opened. A magnet embedded in the back of the cubicle and one embedded in drawer face connect, and the drawer slides out. The box is meant to hang on a wall as a decorative piece, only to be used to hold sacred objects.

Maximilian Greenberg

Untitled (2006)

Walnut
Plywood
Glass
15″ x 28″ x 5″

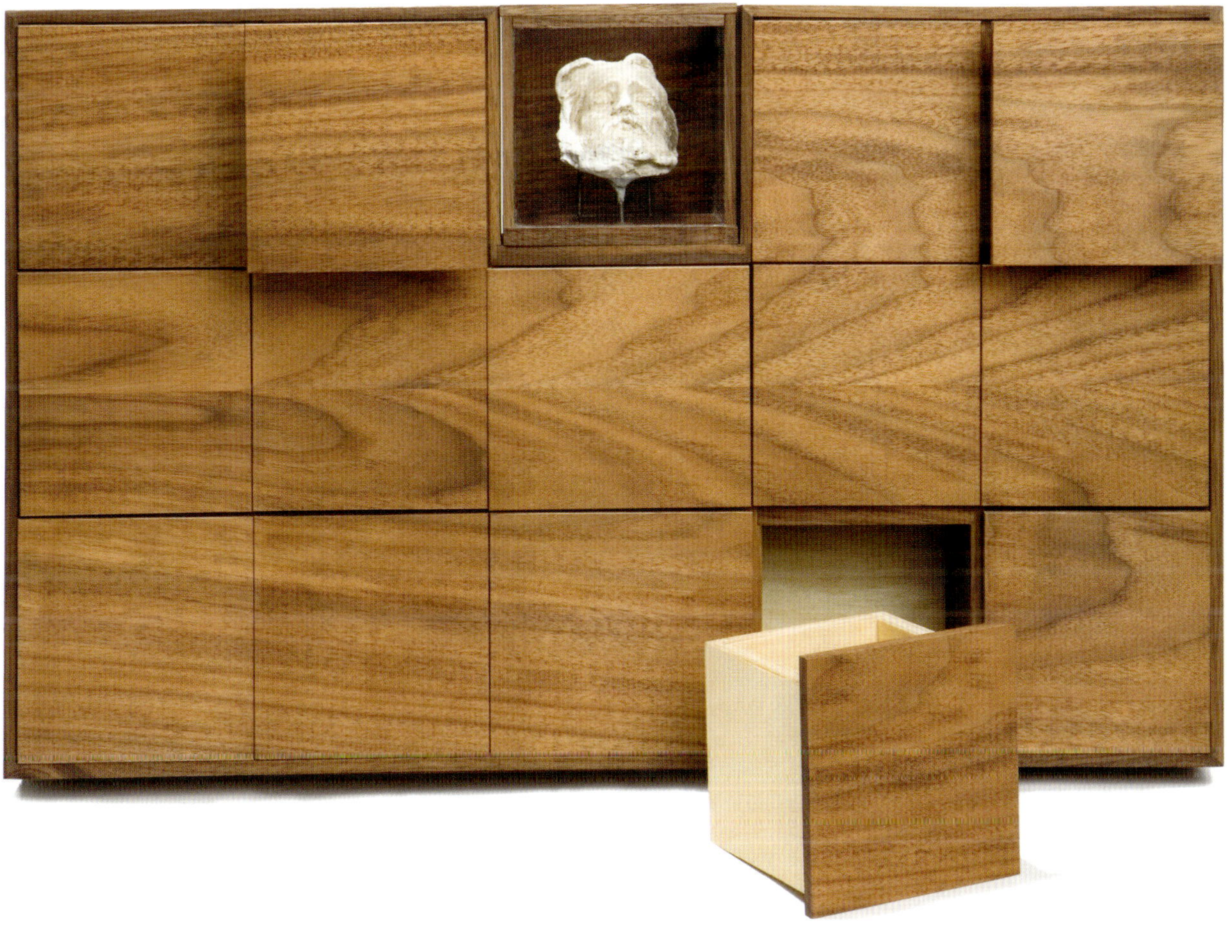

072 MISTERIOS

This piece entwines a doll-like wooden figure within a surreal garment. The branching forms of melted white garbage bags emanate from her and engulf her. By transforming the identity of the material and the artifact, I hoped to create a new, unearthly and magical identity for this formerly discarded object. The inspiration to frame the figure's face came from funerary portraits of nuns at the *Tesoros* exhibit, in which the nuns wore elaborate floral crowns. Like the doll, the portraits of the nuns had a dark and tragic beauty to them that I wanted to recreate in the piece.

Lauren C. Gross

Untitled (2007)

White Garbage Bag (Melted)
16" x 28" x 28"

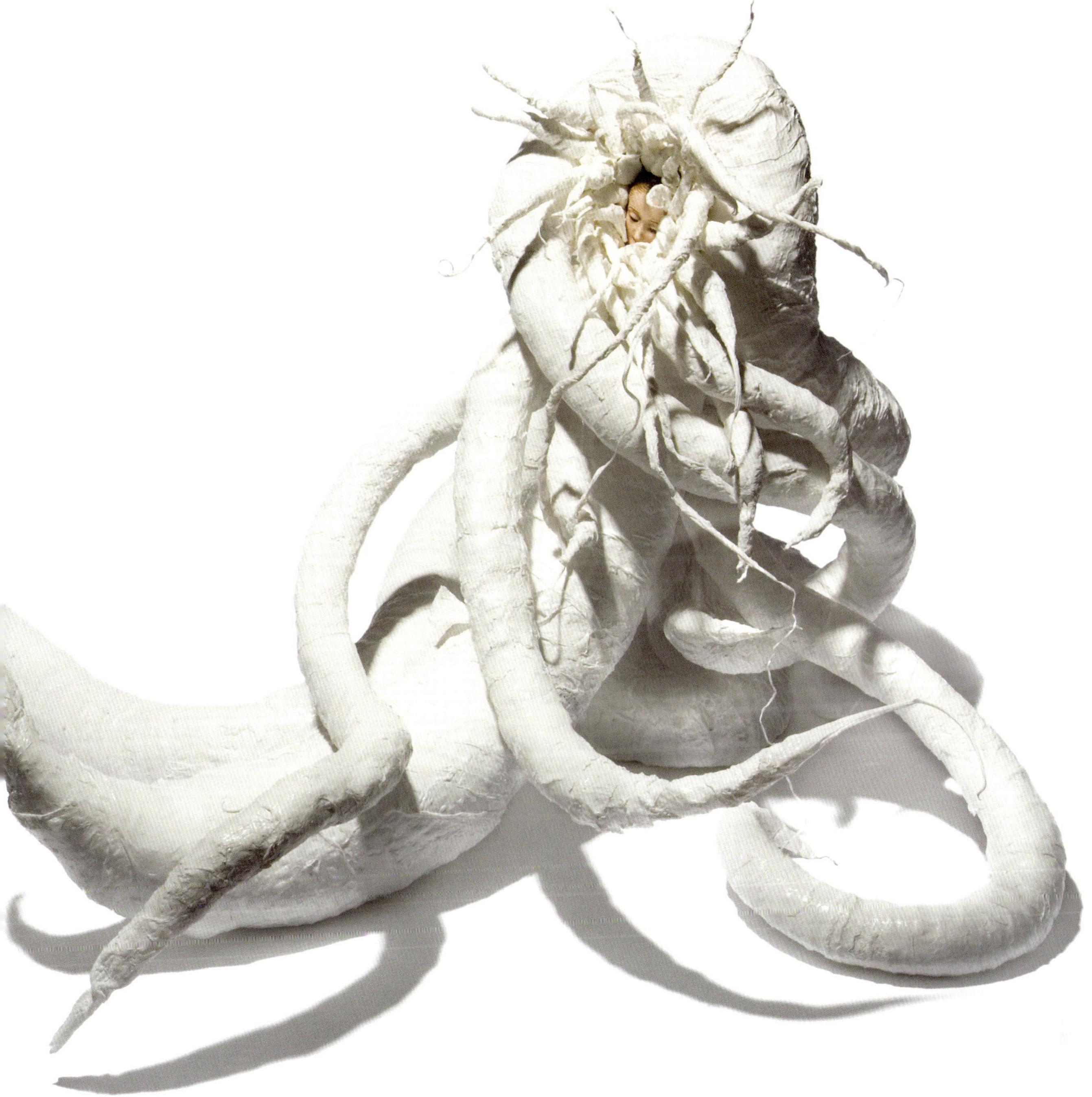

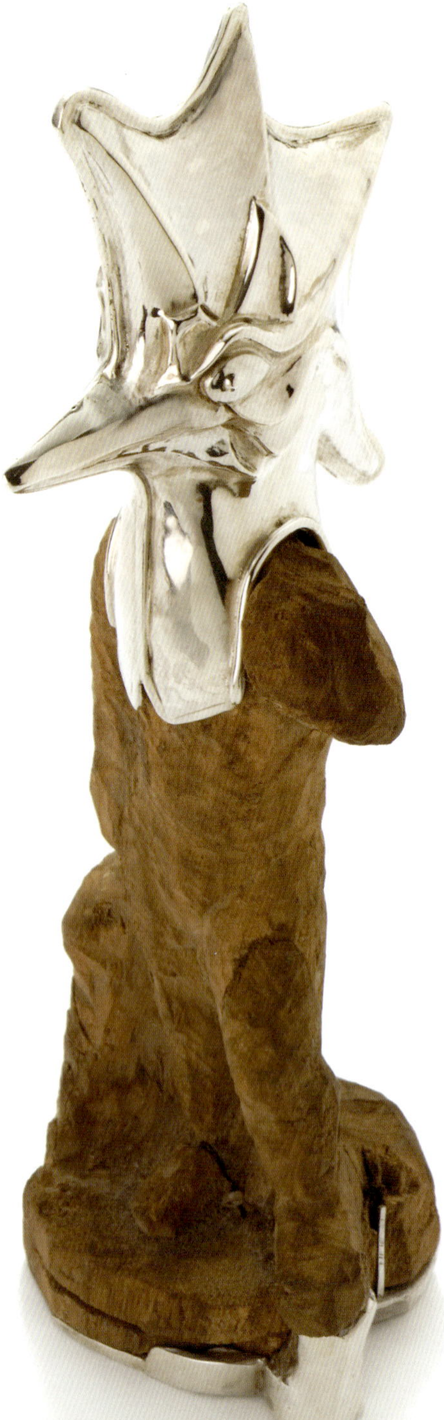

Erin E. Grunstra

Warrior Bird (2007)

Carved Wooden Artifact
Sterling Silver
8″ x 3″ x 3″

strong empowering stature

headless pride

TREASURE

protected   masked   unseen

What is Treasure?

culture
tradition
festival
celebration

Warrior   Warrior Bird

Protecting.

TREASURE

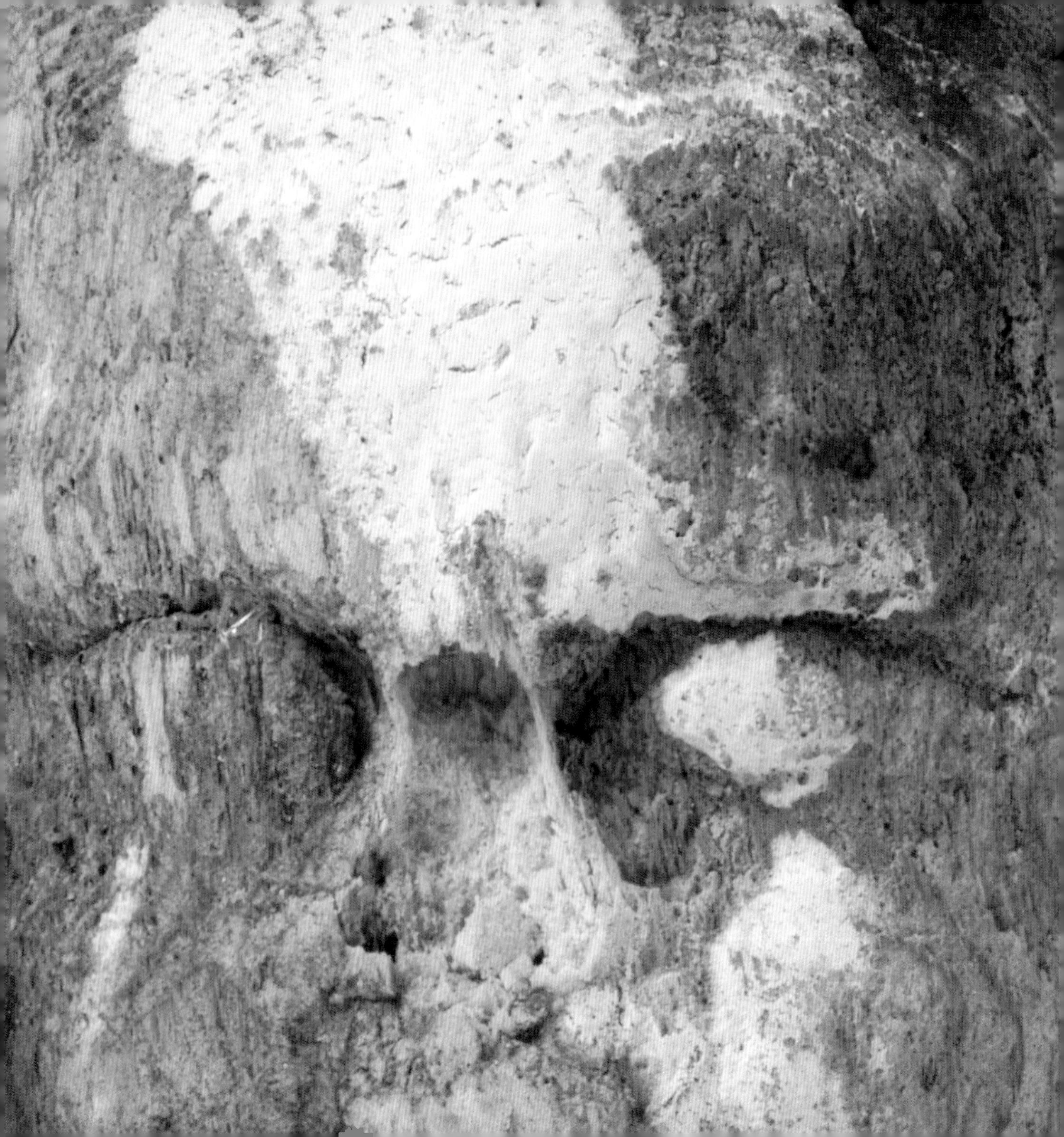

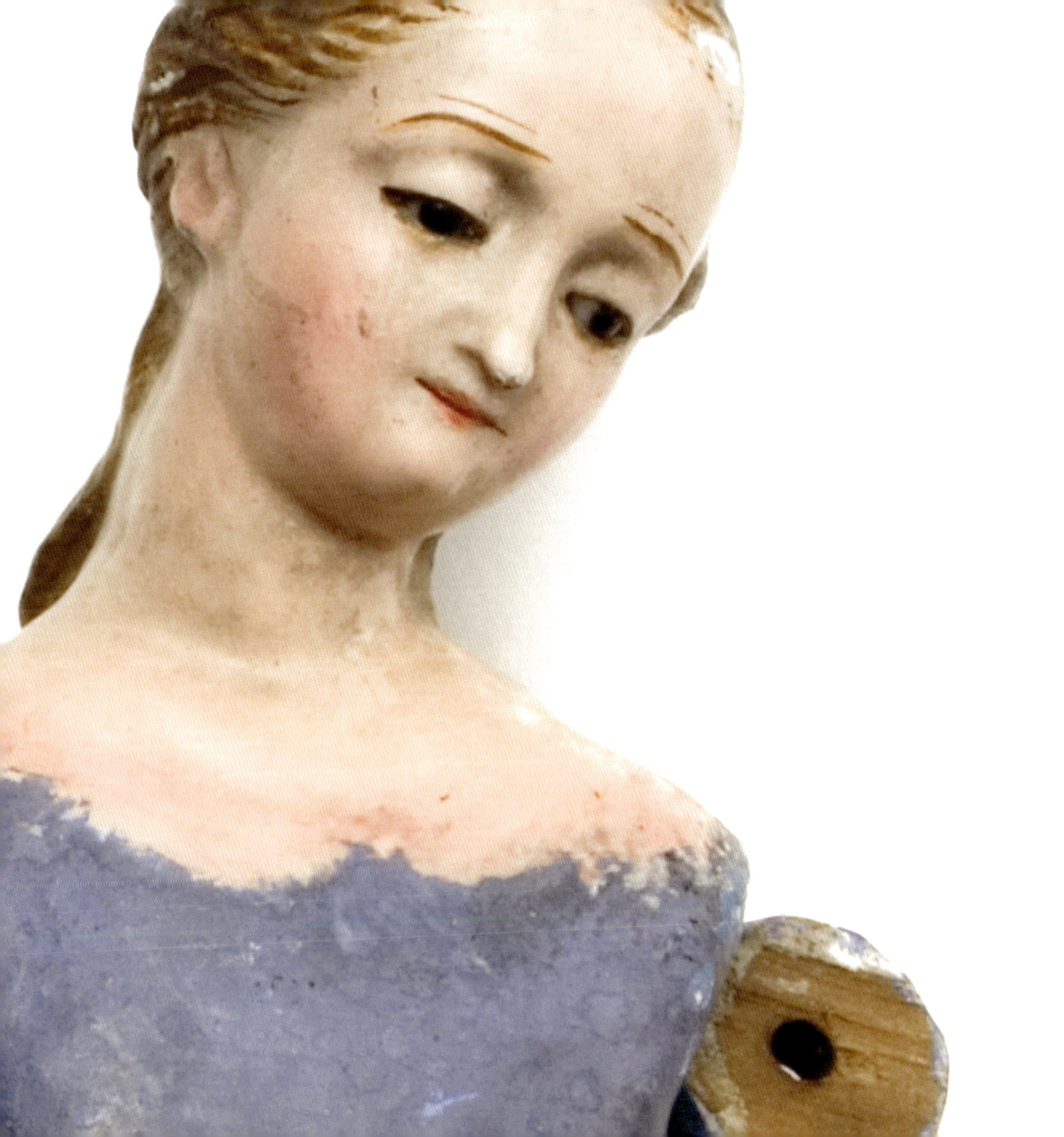

The colonization of Latin America was a turbulent time, filled with violence and death. I imagine people would have wanted to remember and honor those who were lost or displaced during this tumultuous era. I was inspired by the intricate scrollwork in the bronze frame. We use frames to hold items of personal value such as photos of people we care about and want to remember. I am interested in the relationships we create, and how it can be beneficial to carry physical reminders of those who are precious to us. For my *Misterios* piece I replicated the scrollwork of the frame in silver and included my own hair as a part of the design. This brooch is for me to wear as a constant reminder that violence occurs everywhere, throughout time.

Amanda L. Gutsche

Untitled Brooch (2006)

Sterling Silver
Human Hair
3" x 2½" x ½"

Anna S. Ha

My Mask (2007)

Teabags
Thread
34" x 27"

I wear many masks each day. I wear one for my parents, professors, colleagues, friends, adults, children, strangers on the bus, and so on. As a Korean-American woman, I struggle with the many roles that I have cultivated over the years due to the silent demands that have forced me to emphasize or deny certain aspects of myself. When I saw the *Tesoros* artifacts, I was attracted to a porcelain face. I was inspired by the dual symbolism of innocence and purity on the surface, versus the sad history behind the mask due to the colonial oppression in Mexico. I wanted to materialize my own mask out of teabags using origami and the sewing techniques that I have been experimenting with during the semester and plan to explore further in the future. While deciding how to display the piece, I realized that light became essential, because it accentuates the transformation of the material. The front has a smooth geometric design, which is composed as an idealized mask, while the back exposes its hidden supporting nature. I find that, at first glance, the front holds an initial attraction, but the back becomes the truth of the mask and the central point of the piece.

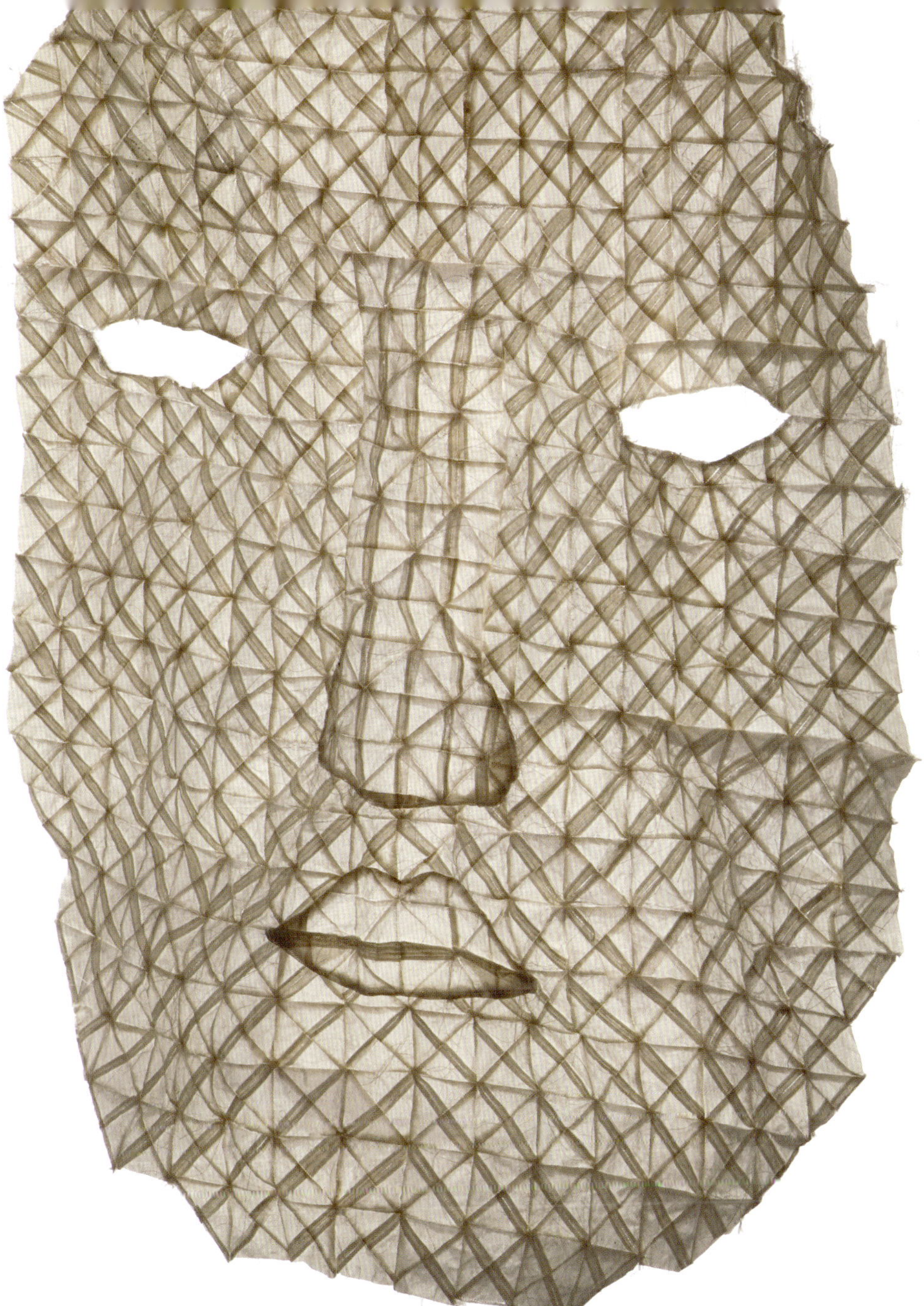

Milagros represent prayers and miracles within Catholic Latin American culture. I was intrigued by their intimate scale and the preciousness that is implied by their gold color and red ribbons. I was particularly interested in the obscurity of some of the images, especially the stomach. My work often involves interior structures of the human body.

Initially, the stomach struck me as an odd image as a source of prayer, resonance, or anxiety. However, the more I investigated my own stomach, internally and externally, I realized the importance of its health and well-being. The stomach is my core, director of nourishment, digestion, and defense. It provides the strength and support for the back and the skeleton as a whole. Mentally, it is inseparably linked with taste, pleasure and survival.

I used my process of sculpting forms from thrown porcelain to create a series of stomach and organ objects. As I worked the small forms in my fingers, the meditative act of creating the stomachs became a parallel to the intention of the original Milagros. The pieces transformed into worry stones or rosary beads. They became a source of releasing anxiety similar to the act of prayer. This imagery and its reference to the human body appeals to my interest in both specimens and science. At the same time, the repetitive process of making is akin to a focused religious practice.

Elizabeth M. Henderson

Core (2007)

Porcelain
Stoneware
Manganese Dioxide
Installation: dimensions variable

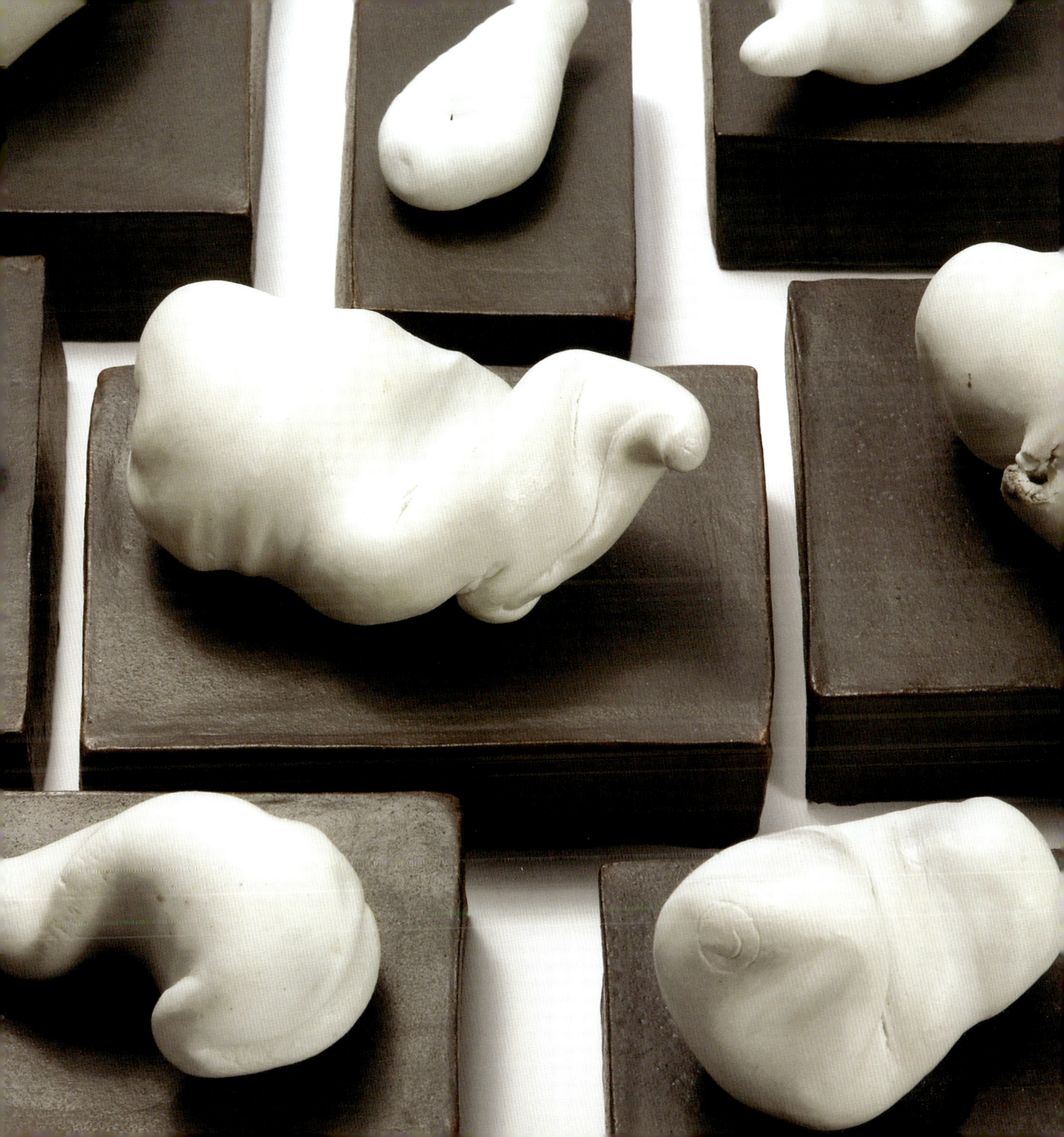

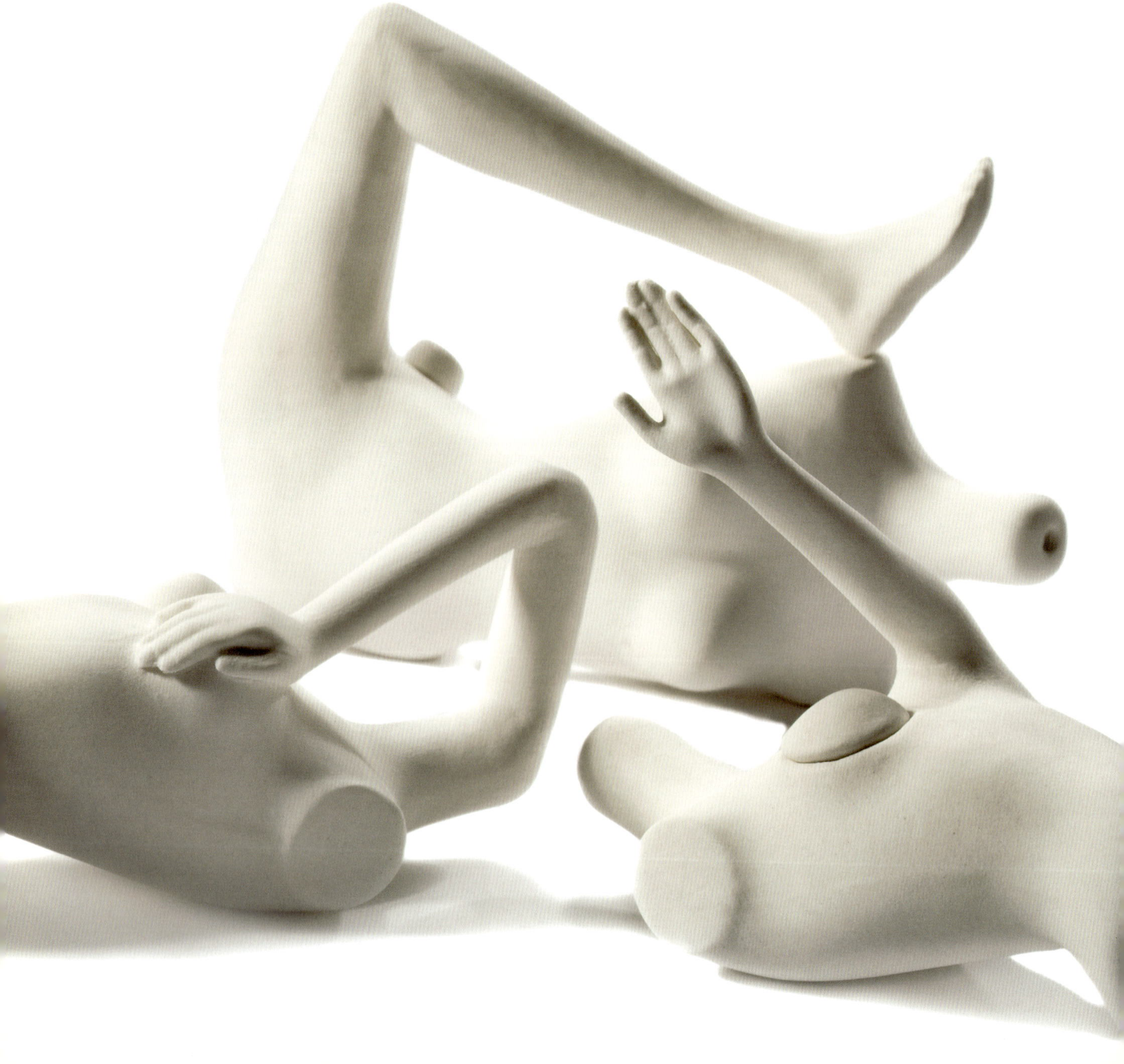

Of all the artifacts, the milagros were the first pieces to capture my attention. I was immediately compelled to rearrange the many small golden pieces into a coherent whole. As I worked with the idea of integration, I incorporated the concept of milagros as prayer, as a means of asking for something better. Since I am not a religious person, I chose to use Barbie, an icon I deem worthy of respect, as the source for my milagros. I took Barbie apart and manipulated her several separate body parts to create a new whole. Through experimentation, I have created a series of interpretations of the milagros that deal with personal health issues. In making these pieces, I have gained experience in mold making and have developed a new conceptual basis for my work that I will certainly use in the future.

Jessica L. Hersh

Barbie Teapots (2006)

Porcelain
3" x 4" x 1" (varied — approximate)

The bust of Christ bearing a crown of thorns inspired these elaborate chalices. In the bust of Christ, thorns are a symbol of commitment, and I wanted to transfer that feeling to the goblets.

The weight of the chalices is intended to place a burden on those who grasp them. Although these chalices are not intended to be religious, the correlation between the thorns and the cup of blood are derived from Christianity.

My work focuses on creating larger pieces through repetition of multiple forms. It is a process that I worked well in this *Misterios* project.

Beth-Ellen E. Hively

Chalices of Thorns (2006/2007)

Hand Built/Thrown Porcelain
Gold Leaf
10″ x 11″ x 11″ (1)
9½″ x 10″ x 13″ (2)

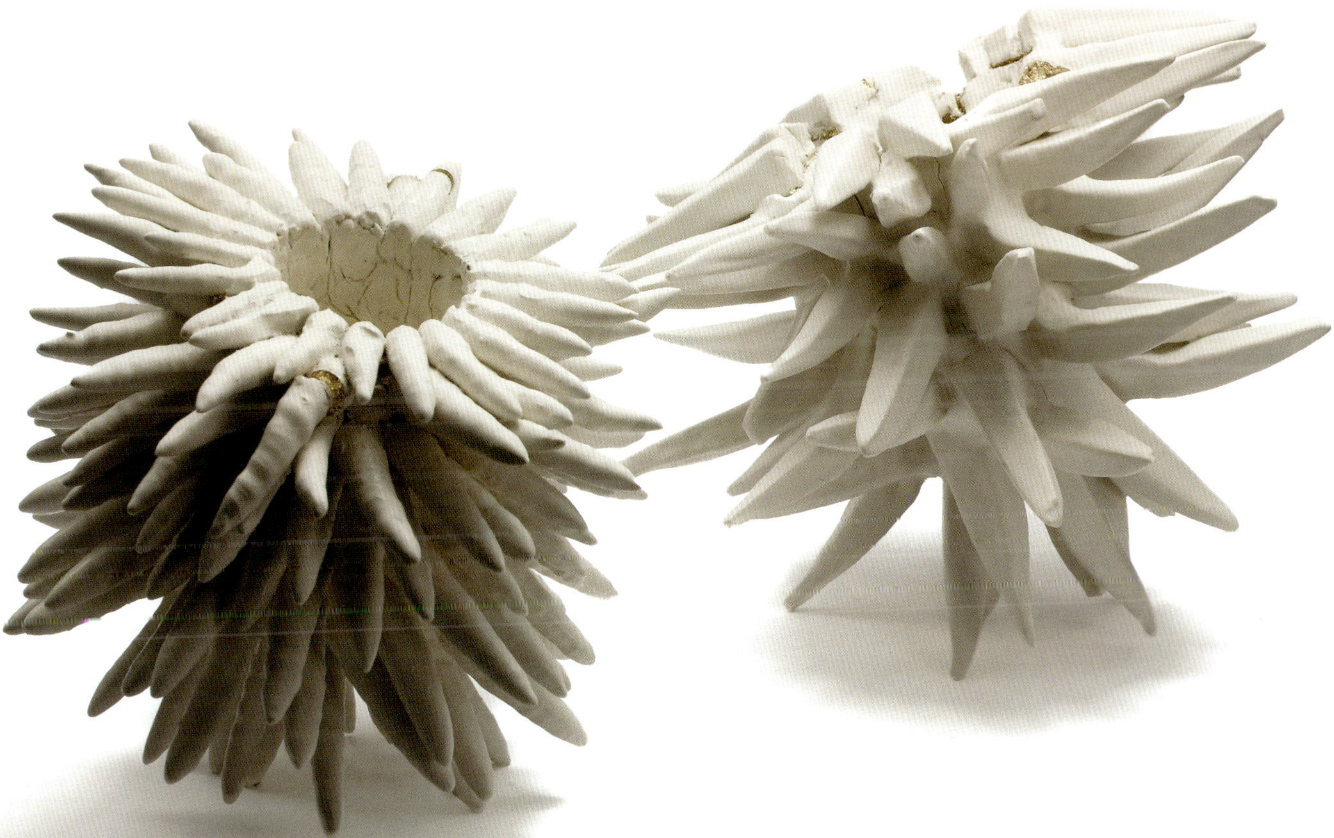

A fascination with collections of small objects made it immediately clear that the milagros would be most inspirational to me. At the *Tesoros* exhibit, the amount of detail and ornamentation in each and every piece was amazing; everything felt so special and sacred. My piece had to replicate that feeling as if the viewer were looking at something too holy to touch.

I blew three glass containers. All the pieces stuffed inside were inspired by popular imagery in Latin American culture: the peppers, flowers and skulls. This project is very much connected to my previous work, especially through the process of stuffing small sculpted forms into blown glass. Also, I was able to push forward ideas for pieces that are completely self-supporting. Trying to display projects more sculpturally without the use of walls and pedestals has always been of interest, so this project enabled the execution of some of these ideas for future work as well.

Sara Horne

Sagrado (2006/2007)

Blown Glass
Steel
Polymer Clay
48″ x 12″ x 12″

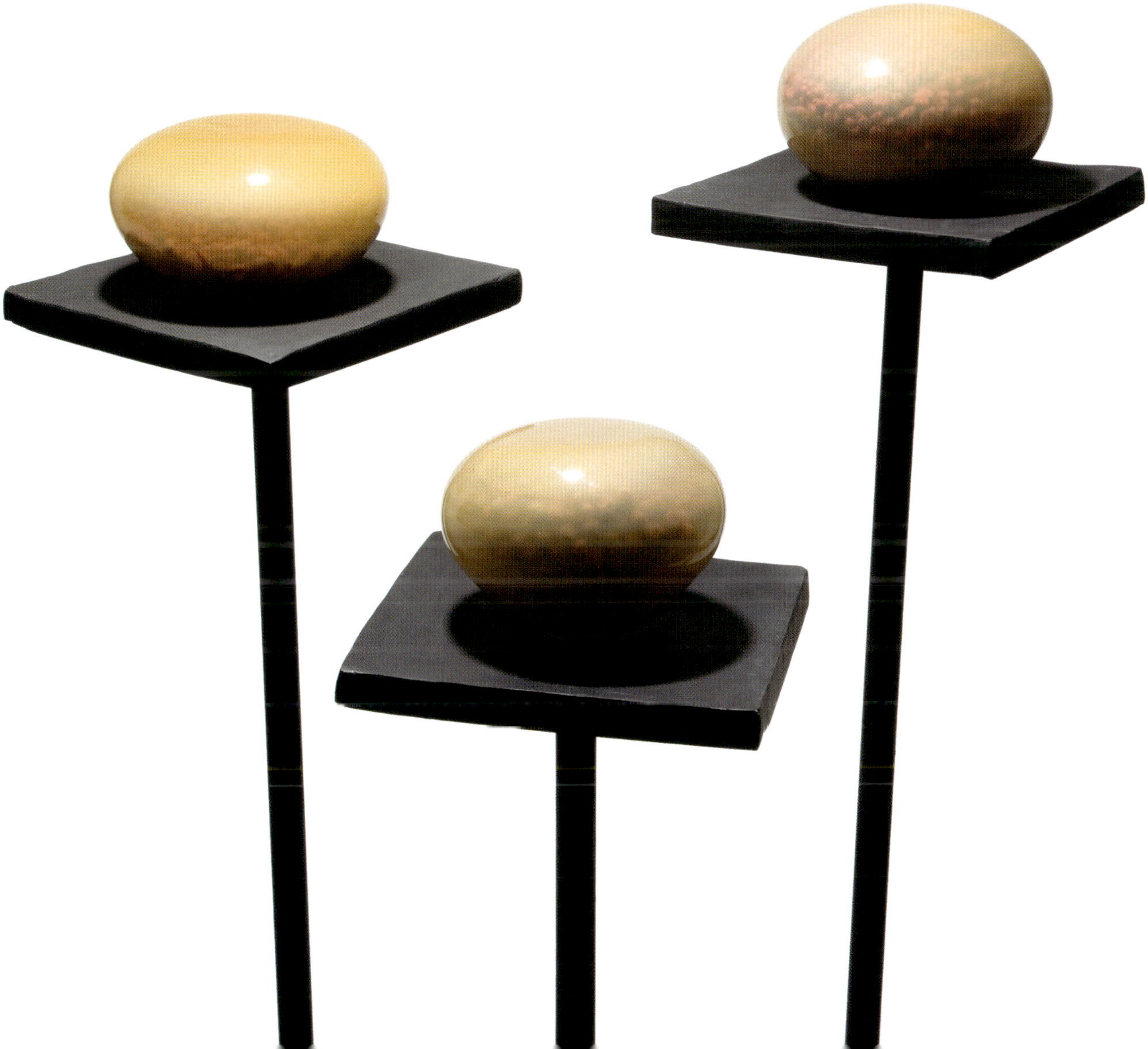

My work consists of functional ceramic pieces that are intended for daily use. I use specific imagery on my surfaces to draw people in, enabling them to make connections to their own lives. I have always been intrigued by human anatomy. Looking at the various artifacts, the milagros immediately spoke to me. I used plaster molds to create my own ceramic milagros and incorporated them into functional ware. The surface imagery served as a tool, unifying the organs and the pot itself. The basis for my glaze choices revolved around colors associated with the body.

The *Misterios* assignment pushed me to think about aspects of my work that I had not considered before. I have now begun to apply three-dimensional forms to my pots. My objective is for people to use these pieces in their everyday lives and to become more aware of their bodies and what they put into them.

Jenna R. Ilconich

Untitled (2007)

Ceramic
13″ x 4″ x 4 ½″

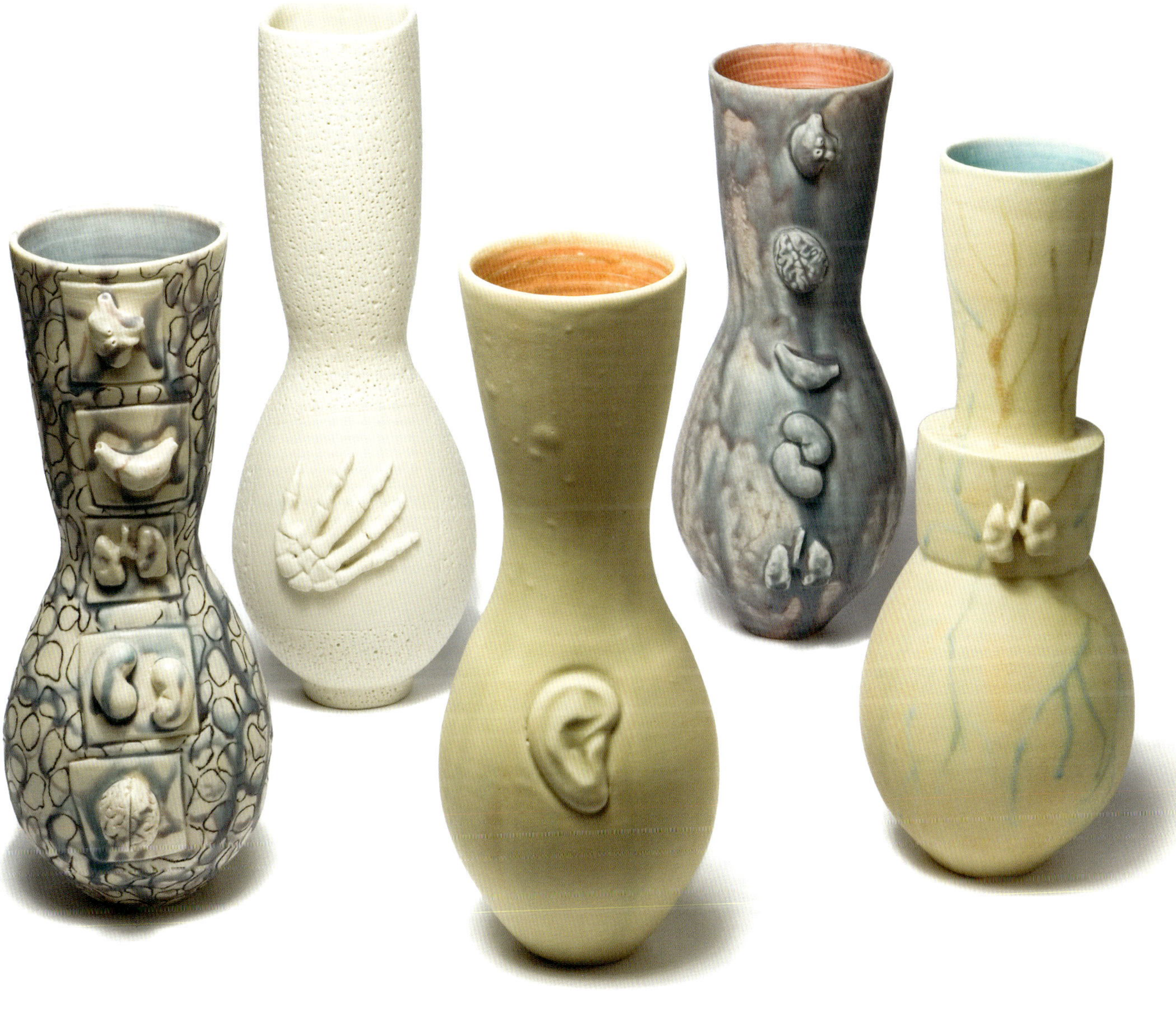

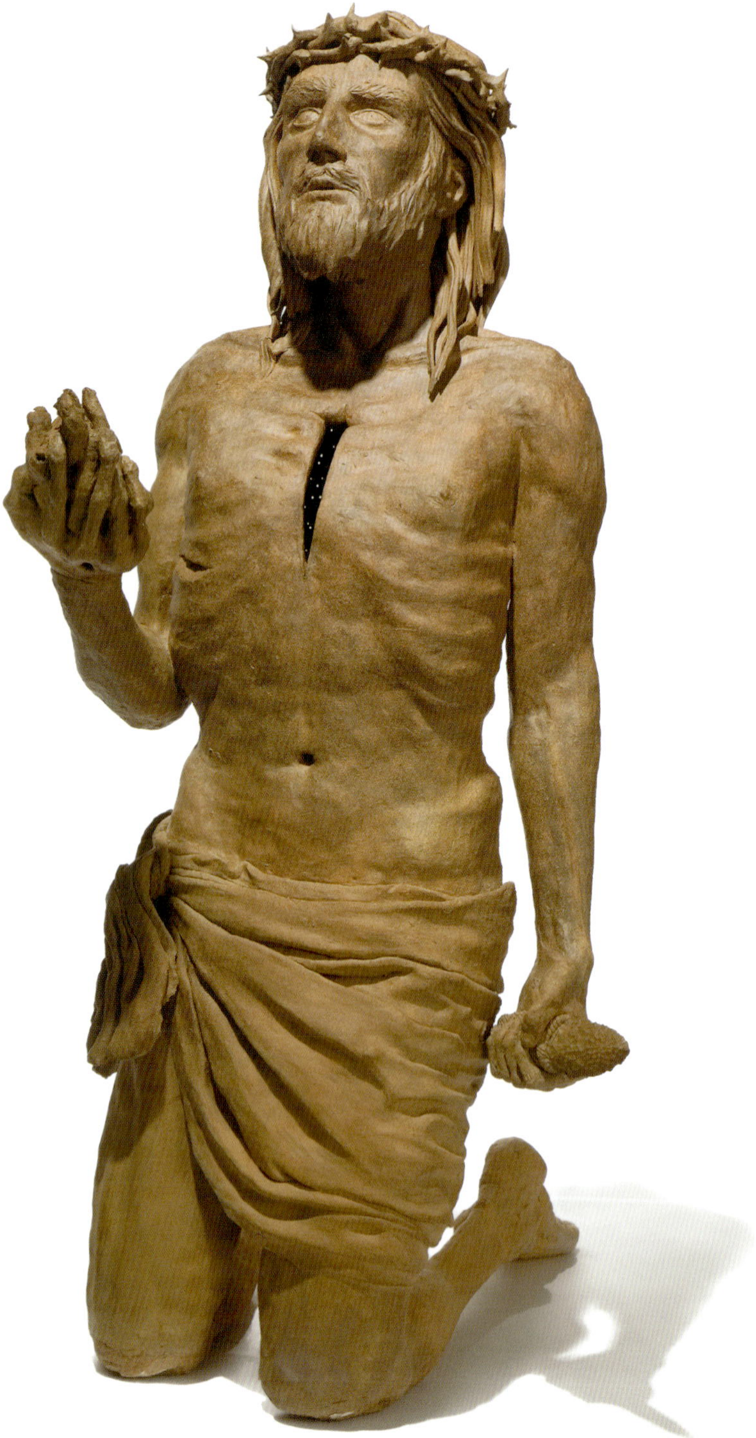

Alexander P. Irvine

The Christ of Reconciliation (2006/2007)

Ceramic
44" x 21" x 33"

When I first saw the Spanish Colonial artifact of Christ depicted with the Sacred Heart, it immediately conjured parallels to Aztec human sacrifice.

Later, I learned that the Sacred Heart was made into an icon for specific veneration by the Catholic Church in the 17th century. This movement was led by missionaries to Mesoamerica who realized that the heart held a significance for the aboriginal people they were seeking to convert. The Sacred Heart icon became an image that was simultaneously revered by Spanish Catholics in Europe and Mesoamericans who saw in it a connection to sacrifices made to the Aztec god of resurrection, Quetzalcoatl.

This icon is a tool used to explain a synthesis of divine concepts in visual terms; Christ is a man, yet omnipresent, sacrificing Himself for the sake of the viewer standing before Him. Christ is holding an obsidian knife, traditionally used by Aztec priests to cut the hearts out of sacrificial victims. The wound creates a window into the cosmos created within Him. This space pierced by light simultaneously represents the fundamental significance of the Messiah's resurrection in Christianity and the cyclical rebirth of the universe in Aztec cosmology. The wounds of the crucifixion are present upon Christ's body as he performs this action to reconcile the foreign idea of Himself within a new cultural context.

Had a communion between these two cultures, resulting in icons like this, been allowed by the workshops producing religious art in Colonial Mesoamerica, it might have converted the aboriginal leap to faith into a leap of faith.

In the Christ of Reconciliation, one can see the icon of the Sacred Heart split into its two primal counterparts to be reborn in a new symbol made flesh.

When I was at the museum exhibition I found myself, surprisingly enough, spending a lot of time looking at the furniture items there. I rather enjoyed the massive wardrobes and cabinets and found the juxtaposition between the brightly painted interiors and drab exteriors curious. At the same time, I was particularly drawn to the baroque styles and curves of the small bronze picture frame. For this piece I wanted to recreate the dynamic contrast between the interior and exterior of these cabinet structures and incorporate the baroque elements from the picture frame to remake the ridiculously oversized structural supports that were seen holding up the shelves in the wardrobe. This piece was largely an exercise in the relationship between inside and out. It looks nothing like most of the other things that I have made, but I feel as though it was a valuable process to further my design sensibilities.

Matthew R. Kelso

Untitled (2006)

Ash
Walnut
Paint
10" x 13" x 21"

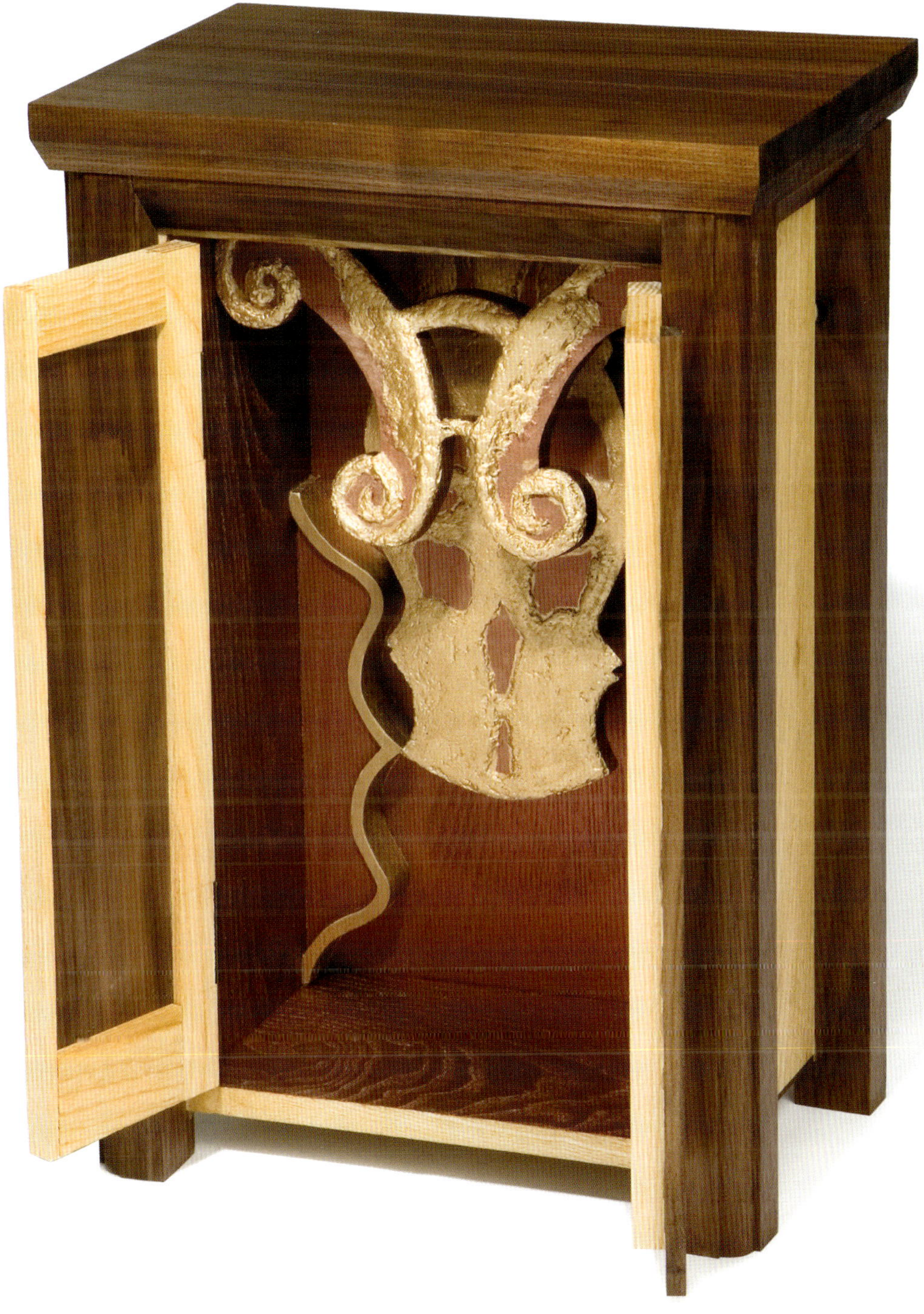

096 MISTERIOS

The contemplative expression on the face of this saint drew me to her immediately. She was made with fine and intricate detail. I decided she needed a reliquary, one that would be made with the techniques and aesthetics common to her time and culture. The chased swirling floral pattern on the arch and the pierced sunburst in the back of the piece are similar to designs found in many items that were made in Colonial Mexico. I made a memorial to give the broken figurine a place to rest and preserve this small piece of history.

Eleanor J. Kennell

Puertas De Misterio (2007)

Wax Figurine Head (Artifact)
Sterling Silver
18K Gold
2 3/4" x 2" x 1 3/4"

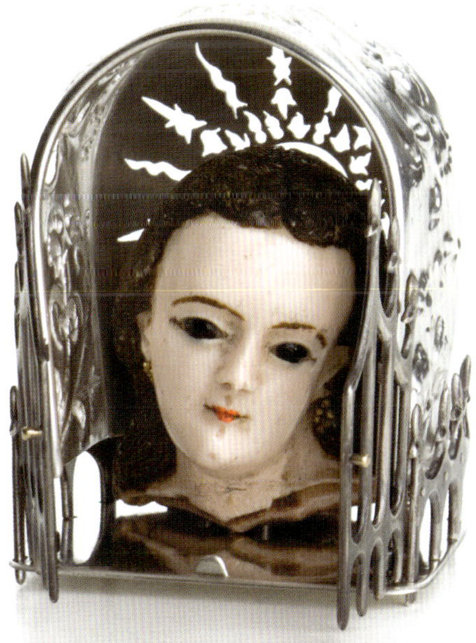

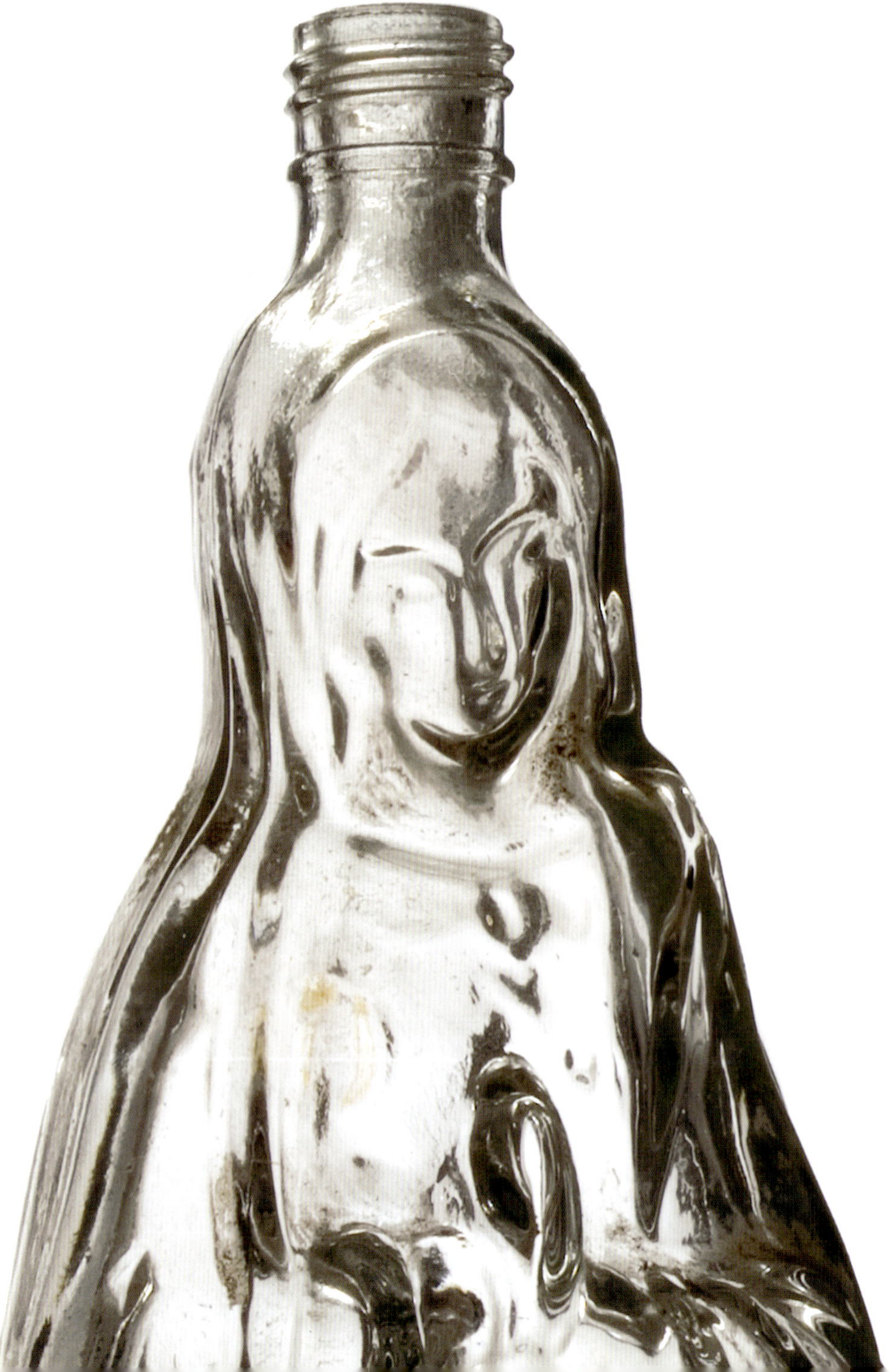

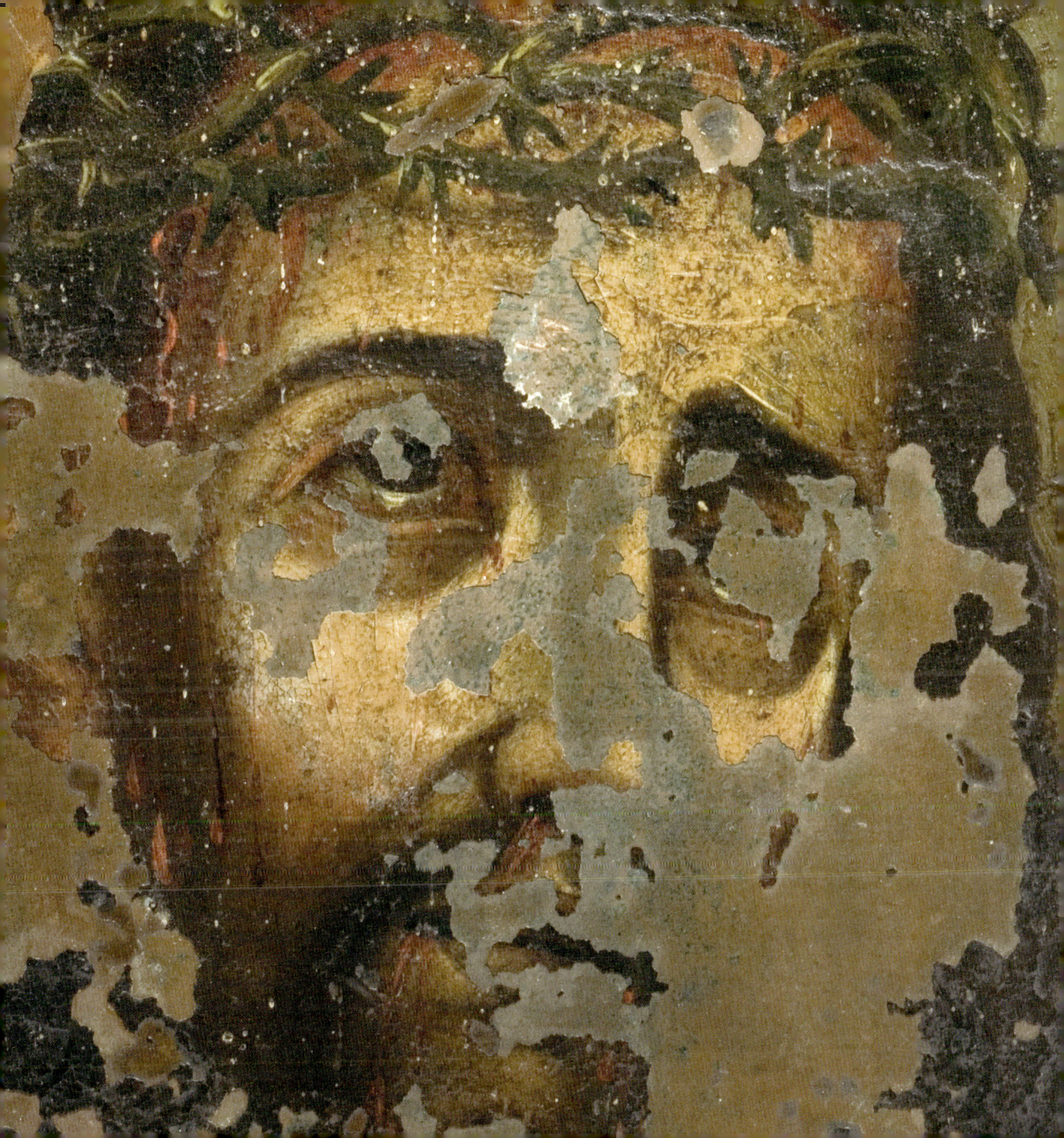

The religious shift from Mesoamerican Paganism to Latin American Catholicism struck me as the most compelling aspect of the *Tesoros* exhibition. I wondered how easily the populace was converted, and how many natives secretly worshipped their own religion in private.

The bronze image of the Madonna and Child reminds me of the iconic image on a scapular, a Catholic neckpiece worn to provide the wearer with the protection of a saint. As a child, the people I was closest to wore scapulars. Not being a Catholic, I often felt like an outsider. My piece is a personal scapular in which my own beliefs are set opposite those represented by the Catholic icon.

Jillian A. Koehnken

Scapular (2007)

Sterling Silver
Bronze
Wool
Rose Plastic
Leather
21″ x 3 ½″ x ⅜″

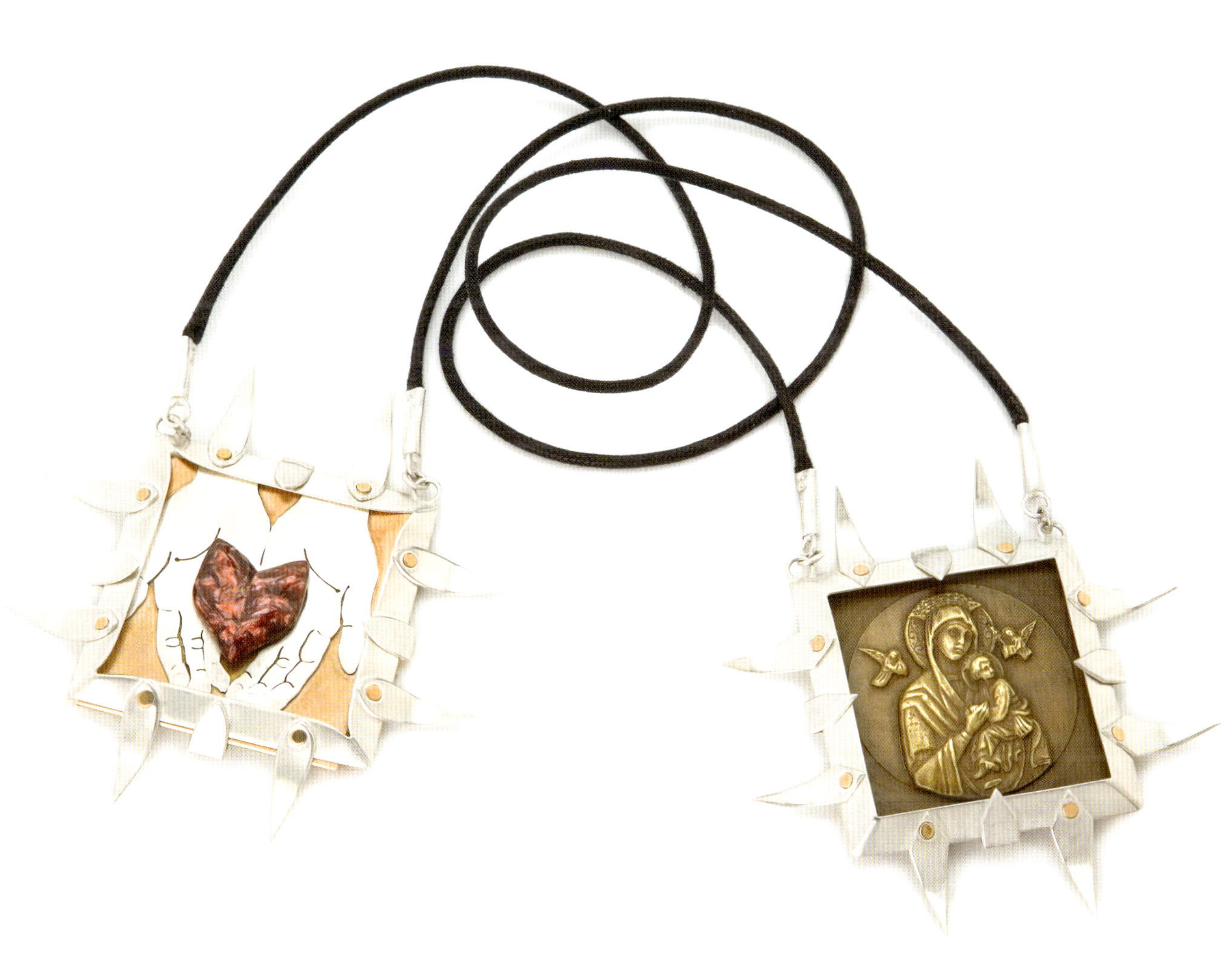

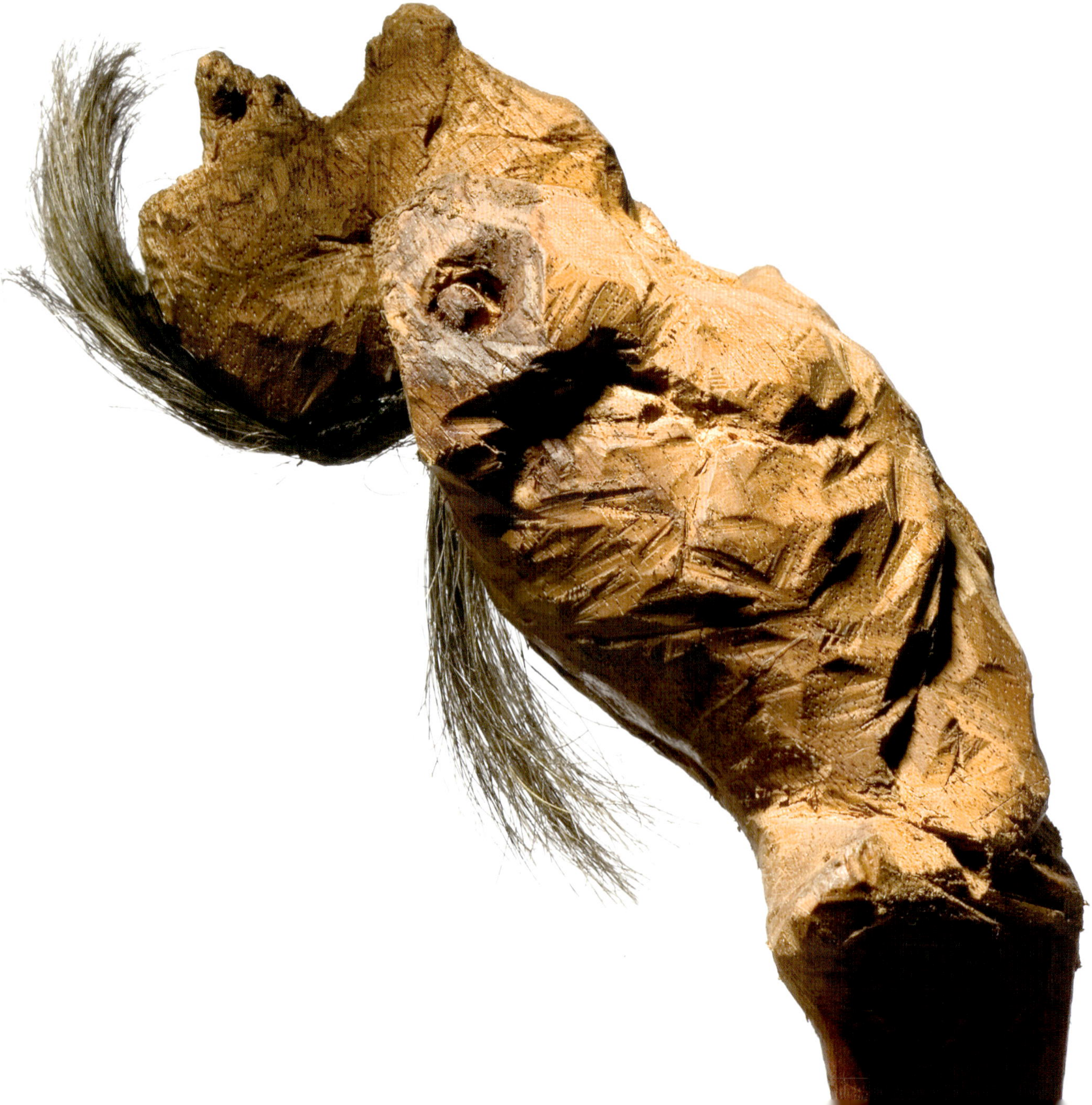

My work is primarily made up of carving, usually based on my figure drawings and executed in the medium of wood. Over the last couple of years I have slowly been developing my carving skills. I enjoy the challenge of translating images and emotional ideas into a three-dimensional piece of work.

My ideas are executed by the intuitive, tactile act of establishing the curved lines and planes of a piece through the gesture of a stroke, whether through use of a pencil, a paintbrush, a knife or a gouge. I have become very attached to creating certain expressive, sincere and deeply personal images and forms which possess great evocative power. Hour upon hour of thought is given to the perspective, placement, gesture and expression of a piece. My art is the instrument I use to translate the fervency I wouldn't attempt expressing in words.

Brittany A. Kurzweil

Untitled (2007)

Mahogany
Bloodwood
Teak
Human Hair
Human Blood
4″ x 2″ x 2″

The iconic image of Jesus and the Sacred Heart speaks of love, devotion, and the willingness to undergo pain and suffering. I was immediately drawn to this particular image because of the rays that emanate out from the heart and onto Him like a protective shield, repelling evil and promoting good.

My own version of a sacred heart relies on eccentric piercing and layering of material to both preserve and contain this precious bronze stamping. Two extravagantly embellished and abstracted metal hearts form a frame around it, topped with a brilliant golden flame. I wanted to reference the beautiful and passionate sense of decoration and devotion that characterizes the Mexican culture. As a brooch, the piece serves as a protective shield worn in the center of one's body, right where you get the dropping, squeezing, pulsating feeling during moments of anxiety.

Lauren A. LeBlanc

A Valentine for Jesus (2007)

22K Yellow Gold
Sterling Silver
Aluminum
Bronze Artifact
7″ x 4 x ½″ (brooch)
8½″ x 5½″ x 3″ (Closed Box)
8½″ x 12½″ x 3″ (Open Box)

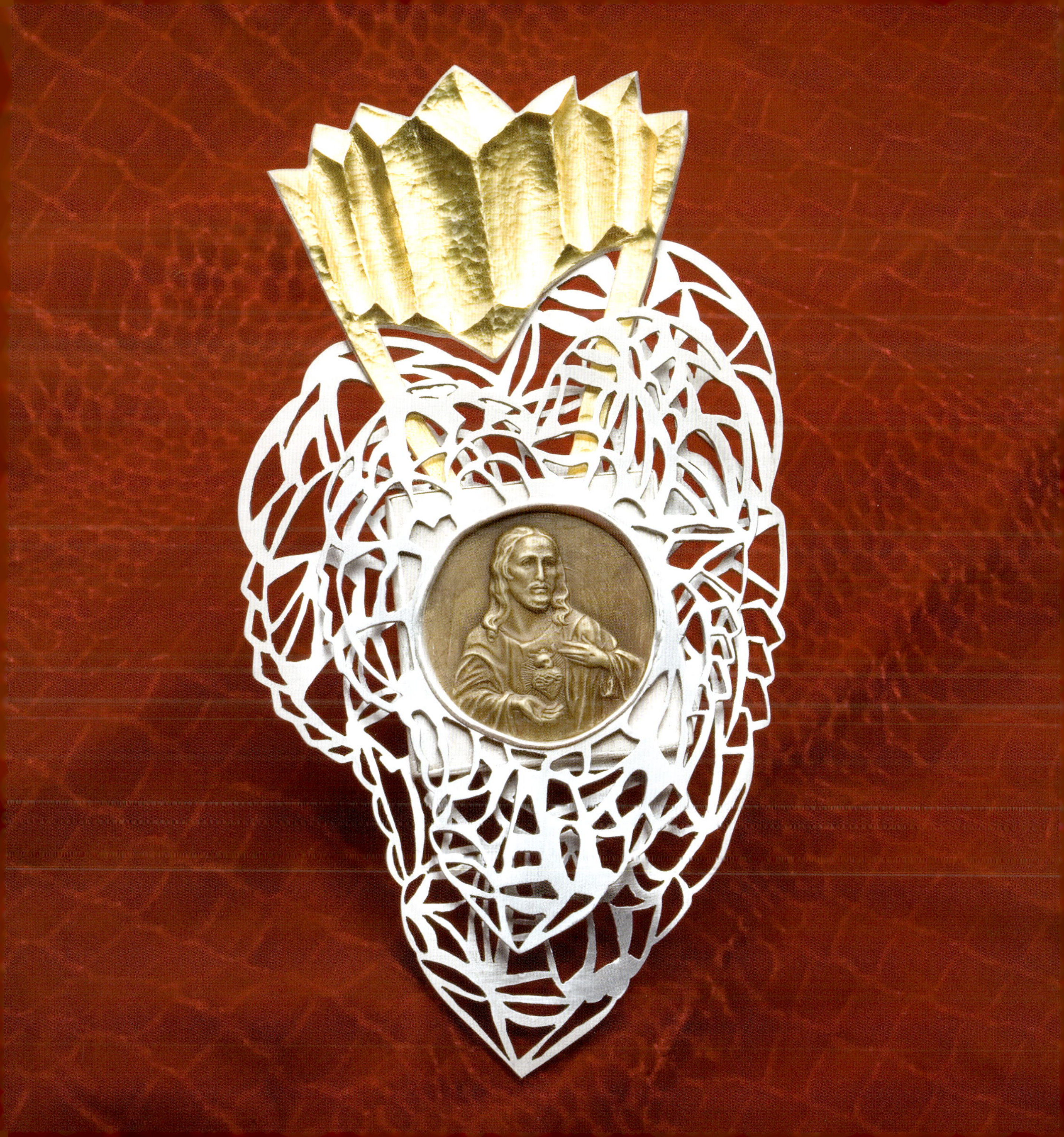

What was most striking about the bronze frame is its ornate beauty. It is an object, or treasure, composed of baroque embellishments created to hold a painting, most likely a religious work or a portrait similar to those we saw at the *Tesoros* exhibit. What I found most intriguing about this frame is its emptiness, and the possibilities of what could have gone inside of it. What I wanted to do with my piece was utilize the aesthetic qualities to create a piece that has a similar aspect of mystery, beauty and baroque elegance. I used the techniques I have cultivated over my time at school to sew together an expressive piece of fabric made of bronze mesh and thread. I wanted my piece to reflect the imagery I saw in the exhibit and in the frame itself, but I also wanted it to become a manifestation of my own spirituality and of my artistic journey. This piece is only a framework, a structure that can become so much more or so much less, depending on who looks inside.

Amanda L. Lewis

Glory Hole (2007)

Bronze Mesh
Wire
Artificial Sinew
12″ x 12″ x 64″

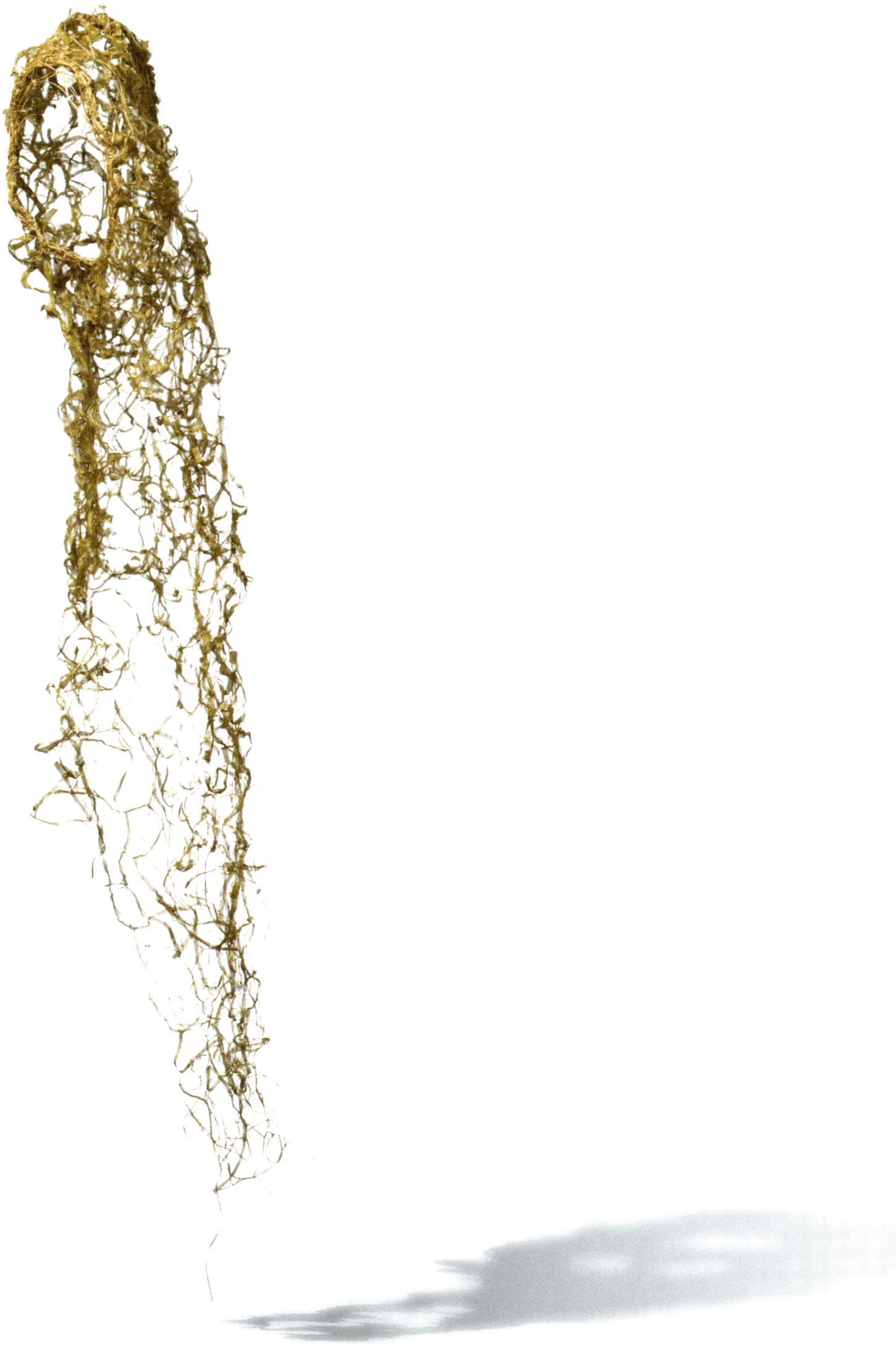

Colin J. Lusis

Holy Water Vessels (2006)

Blown Glass
Spun Brass Wire
Fiberglass
Baking Soda
7–9″ x 2½–3″ (approx.)

The artifact in the *Tesoros* exhibit I was drawn to was the blown glass Virgin Mary used to hold Holy Water. In researching the bottle, I found the many different uses of holy water interesting and it inspired me to create individual vessels for each application. Having worked in glass series earlier in the semester, I decided to create multiple forms with separate surface treatments. Using spun brass wire, fiberglass, baking soda and water, each surface is unique while the overall form represents the gestured praying position signifying its religious nature.

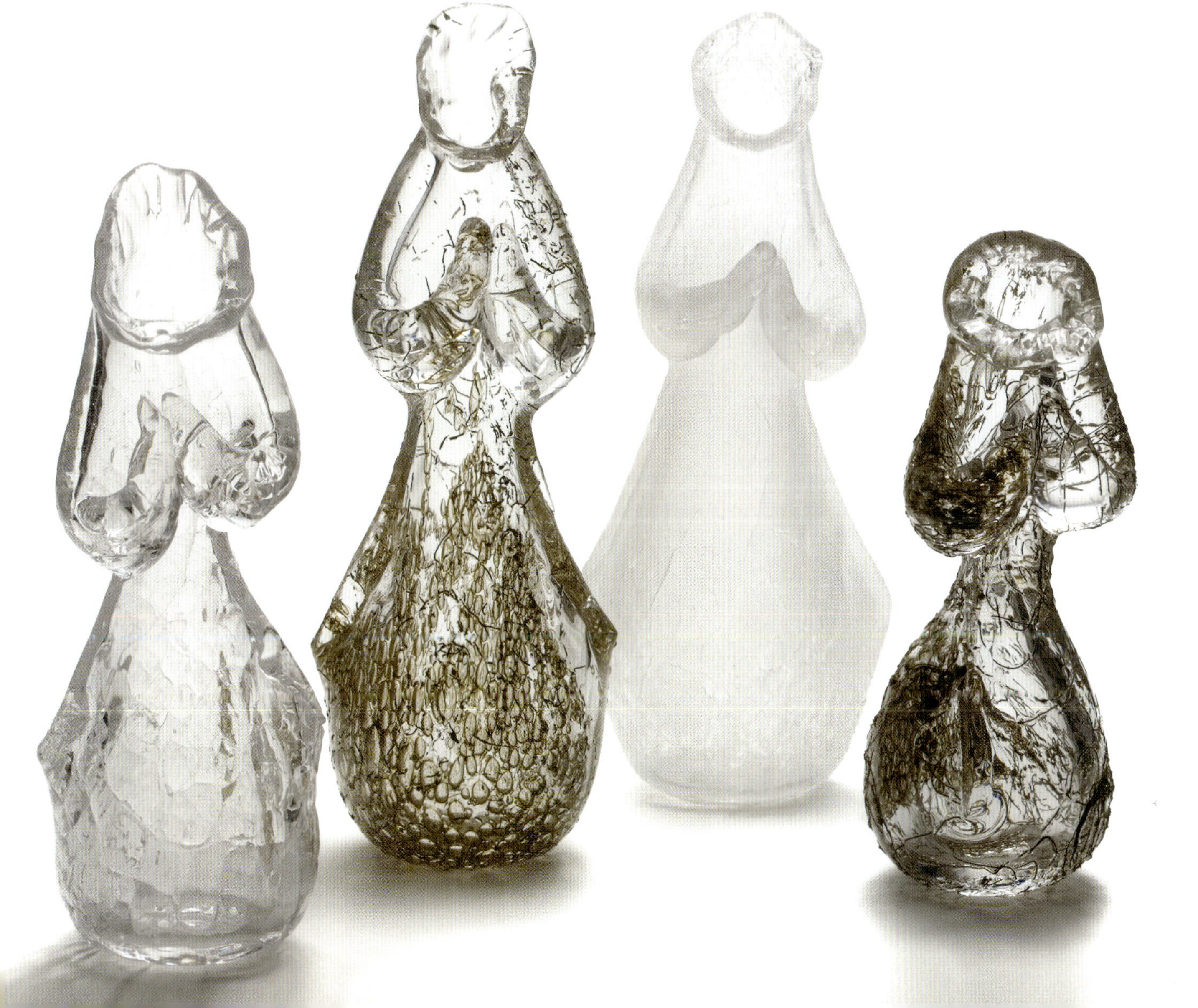

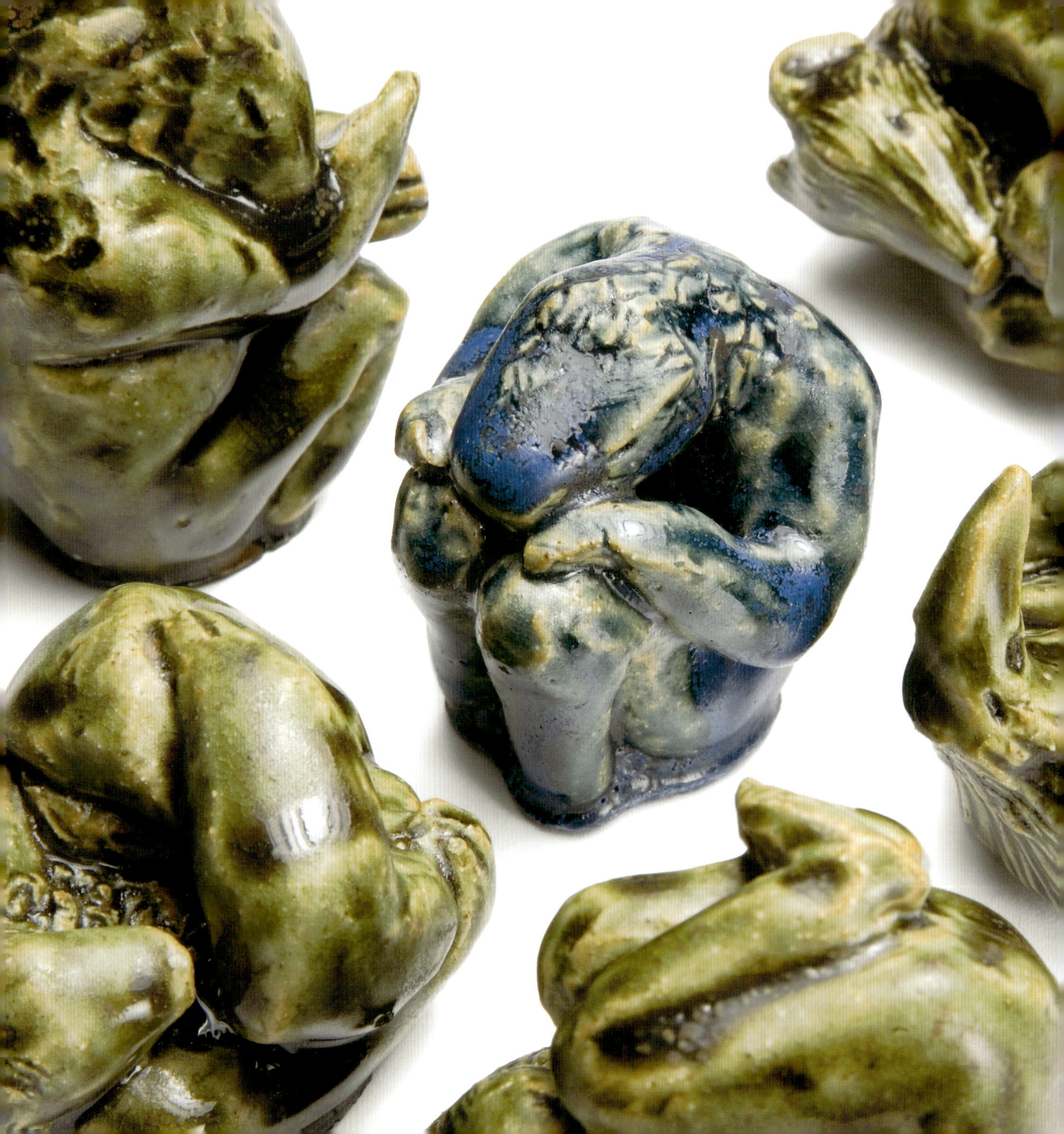

During the colonization of Latin America, shrines to saints were built on top of older religious sites, and the miracles and powers previously ascribed to the local "pagan" god were given to the Christian saint. I was drawn to create icons of these older gods. I wanted to show that the indigenous religion had been co-opted by Christianity. It had never really been erased; it simply faded into the background.

My imagery was inspired by the small gold milagros, or miracle charms. In Latin America, milagros are given to images of saints as thanks for solving problems. In my work, I often focus on animal imagery. For this piece, I blended animal imagery with human forms, referring to the global proliferation of human-animal hybrids as religious figures. This project challenged me to be more expressive and inventive, giving me the opportunity to grow exponentially as an artist.

Andrea C. Manning

Small Gods (2007)

Glazed Stoneware
1 1/2–3" x 1 3/4–2 3/4" x 1 1/2–1 3/4"

Margie M. Manogue

Three Cups and Saucers (2007)

Porcelain
6 ½" x 7 ½" x 5"

As inspiration for my work, I used the wooden polychrome torso of Jesus. This is not because of its religious content, but because I use the human figure in much of my work. It was not until later, in the conception of this piece, that the religious aspect of *Tesoros* inspired me. Many of the *Tesoros* objects were based on Catholicism and crafted by extremely devout religious believers. Being that I am spiritual but don't subscribe to one particular religion, I decided to take the male figure of Jesus and transform it into something I felt more familiar and comfortable with—the figure of a woman. To me, the deity seems to be a feminine force, whether it be mothering, childlike, or somewhere in between. Because I have a firmly rooted belief that craft should be functional, I have separated the form into cups and saucers. Wheel throwing is a process that is crucial to my work, thus this piece is made up of multiple parts that I have thrown and assembled. Using high-fired porcelain without glaze represents the purity of the female form and conveys the divinity of these bodies that act as vessels. I decided to make three of these cups and saucers to represent the Holy Trinity, which was an important image in the Mexican Baroque period.

This process was a very personal exploration of my own opinion, beliefs and aesthetics that has allowed me to learn more about who I am as an artist.

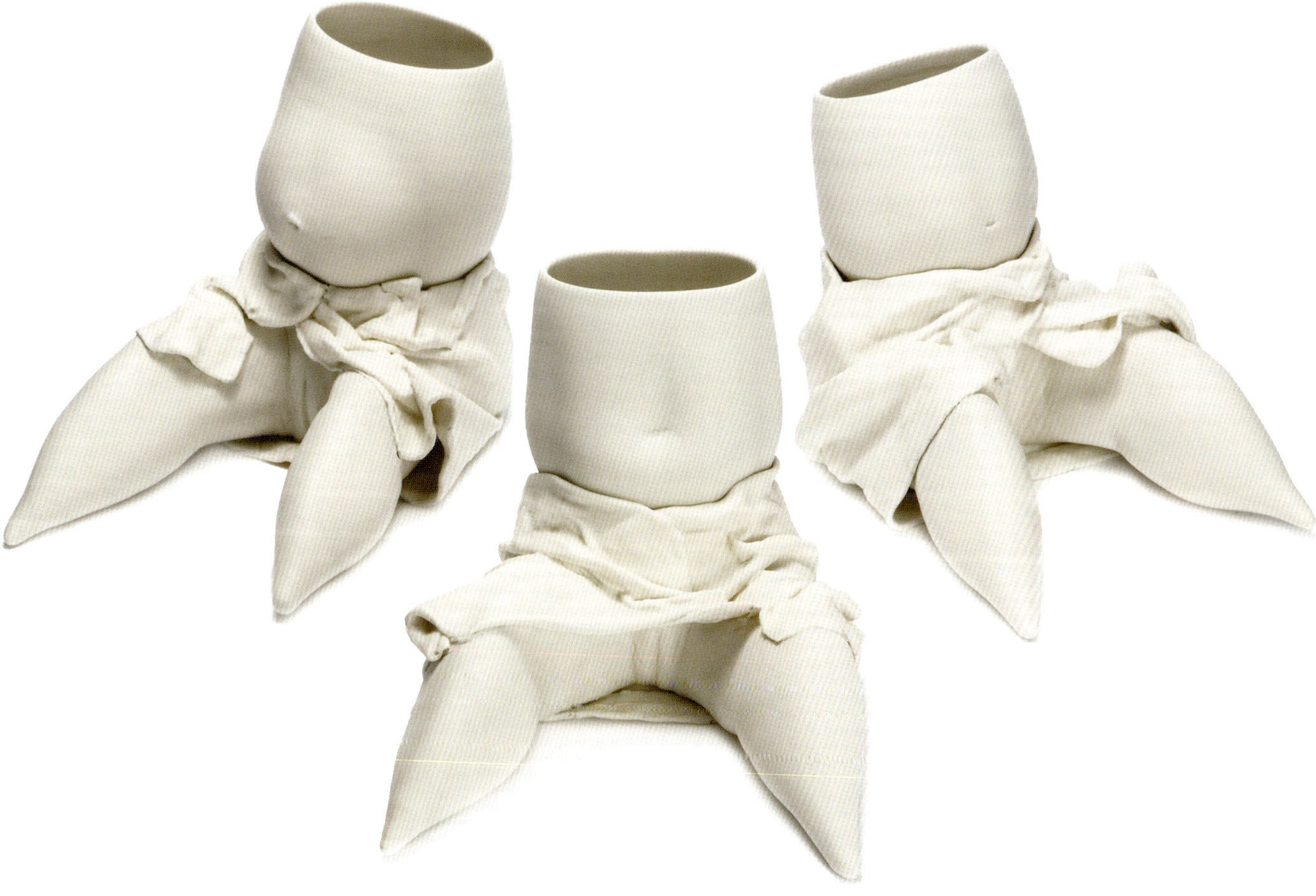

Aside from occasionally attending the local Unitarian Universalist church and celebrating a combination of Hanukkah, Winter Solstice and Christmas, organized religion was almost completely absent from my childhood. In school, I learned about the history of Western Civilization, the wars, crusades and massacres connected with the church, and the prominence of religion in art history. While it was challenging to complete a project heavily imbued with religious imagery, it also compelled me to consider the role of religion in the sublimation and oppression of one culture by another, and how that may be contained within art.

I was inspired to work with two wax heads, assuming they were depictions of two religious icons, Mary and Jesus. Each was replicated on the 3-D printer, enabling me to cast my own versions in wax to create multiple objects evocative of candles. I was drawn to the idea of a candle because it represents light and dark, hot and cold, life and death. The ambiguous nature of such opposites mirror my feelings about religion.

Just as candles are used in vigils for the dead, these heads are a symbolic body count for lives lost over centuries of religious conflict. I do not intend for these objects to be melted, but rather to allow their long wicks and visceral red coloring to suggest poverty, illness, suffering and loss of life.

What are the repercussions of an entire civilization converting to one religion? When a candle burns to the end of its wick, what is left behind?

Emily R. Moroz

Fieltro (2007)

Cast Wax
Dyed Cotton String
Found Objects
14″ x 72″ x 3¼″

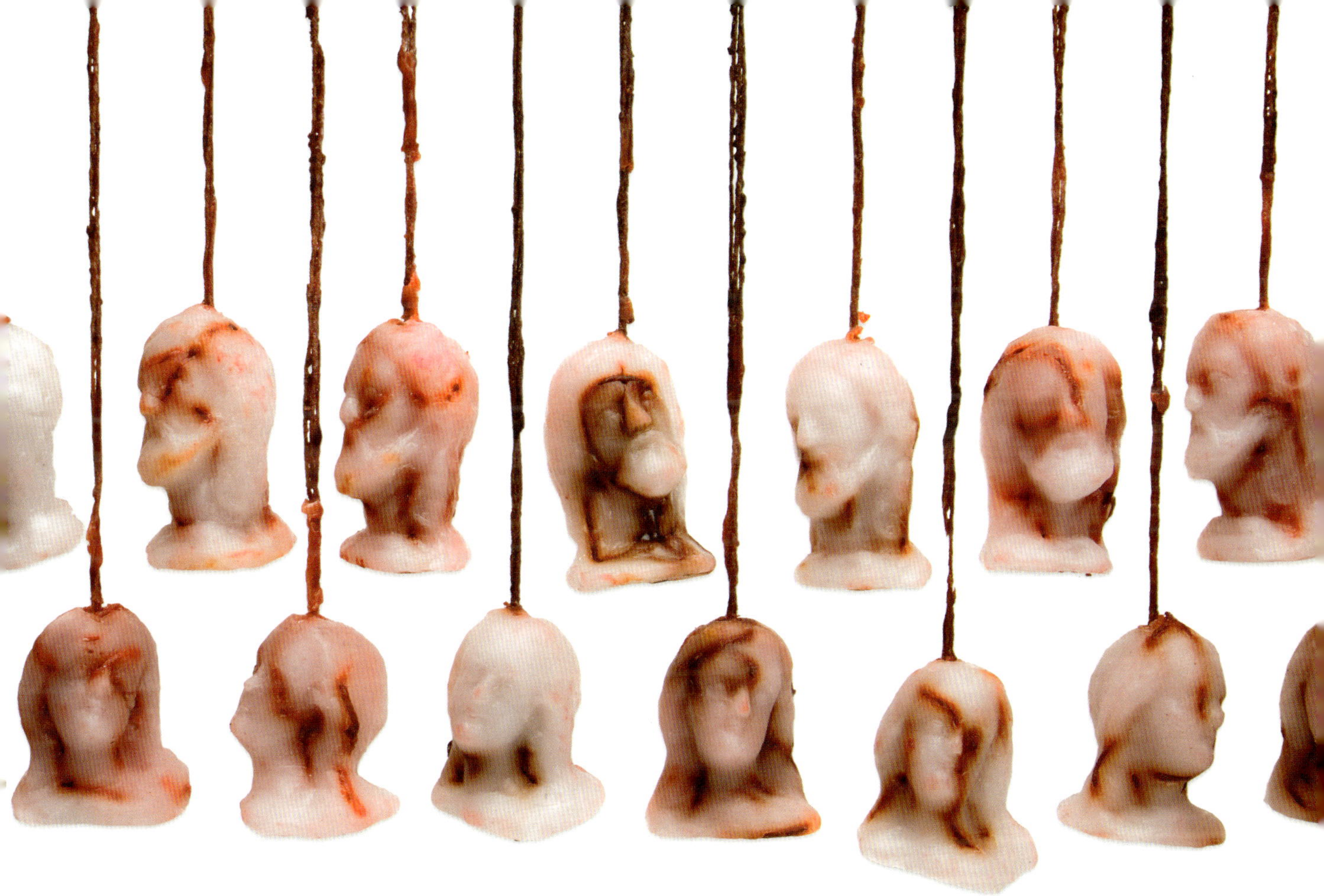

I was drawn to several strap hinge trunks and writing desks in the *Tesoros* exhibition at the Philadelphia Museum of Art. Fascinated by the technical construction and use of materials in these works, I was inspired to employ a similar approach to make this coopered box. I wanted to create a kind of visual metaphor referencing the upheaval, destruction and religious fervor that characterized the colonization of Latin America during the 15th and 16th centuries. The Catholic mandate to convert the natives was based in a purity of religious thought, but in reality it employed fear, violence, greed and deception to its own ends. My goal was to express these ideas through the clean, pure construction of a wood chest and the deception of its appearing to be a locked box.

Jamie B. Newman

Coopered Chest (2007)

Mahogany
Bending Ply
12" x 9" x 10 3/4"

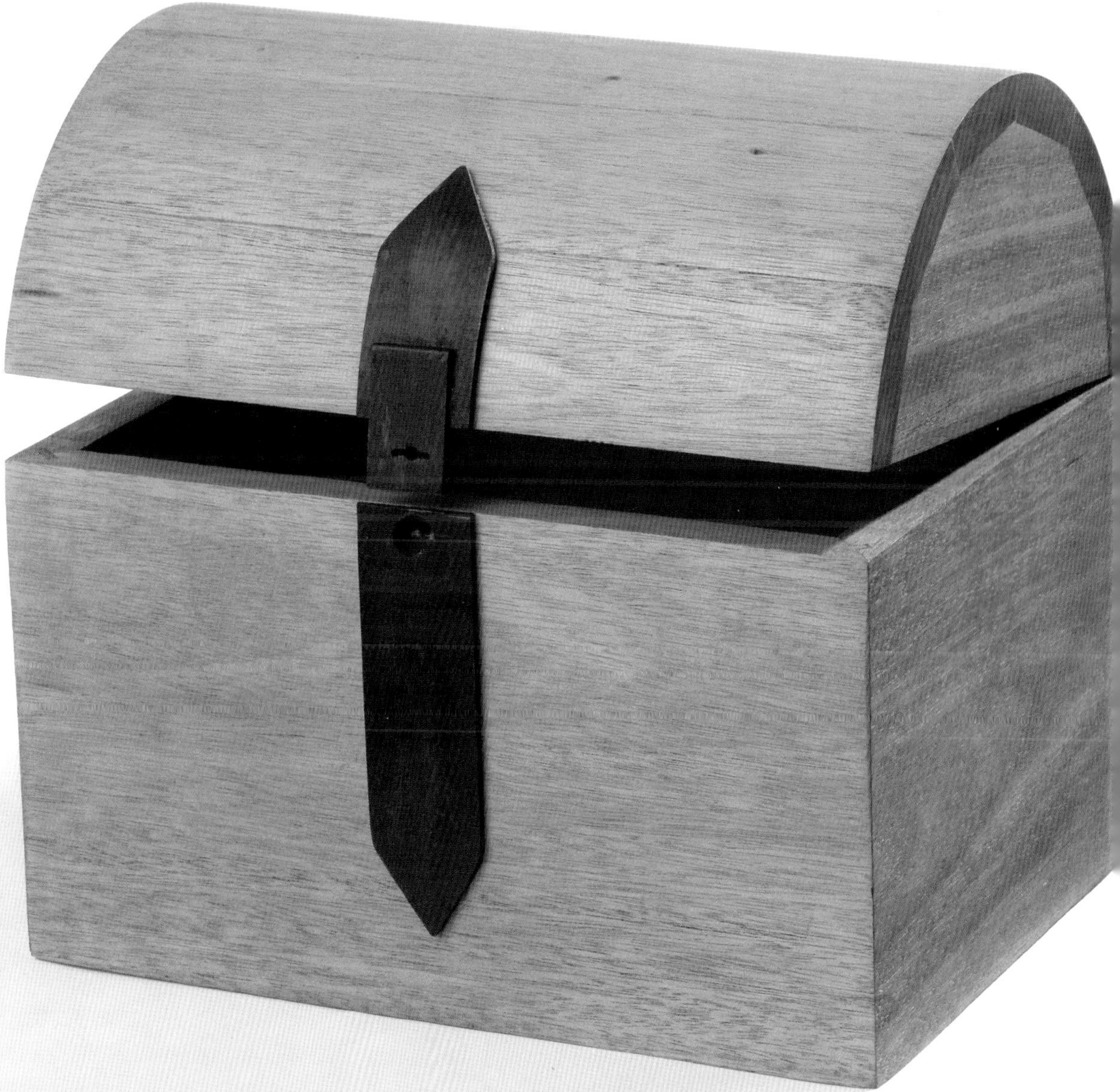

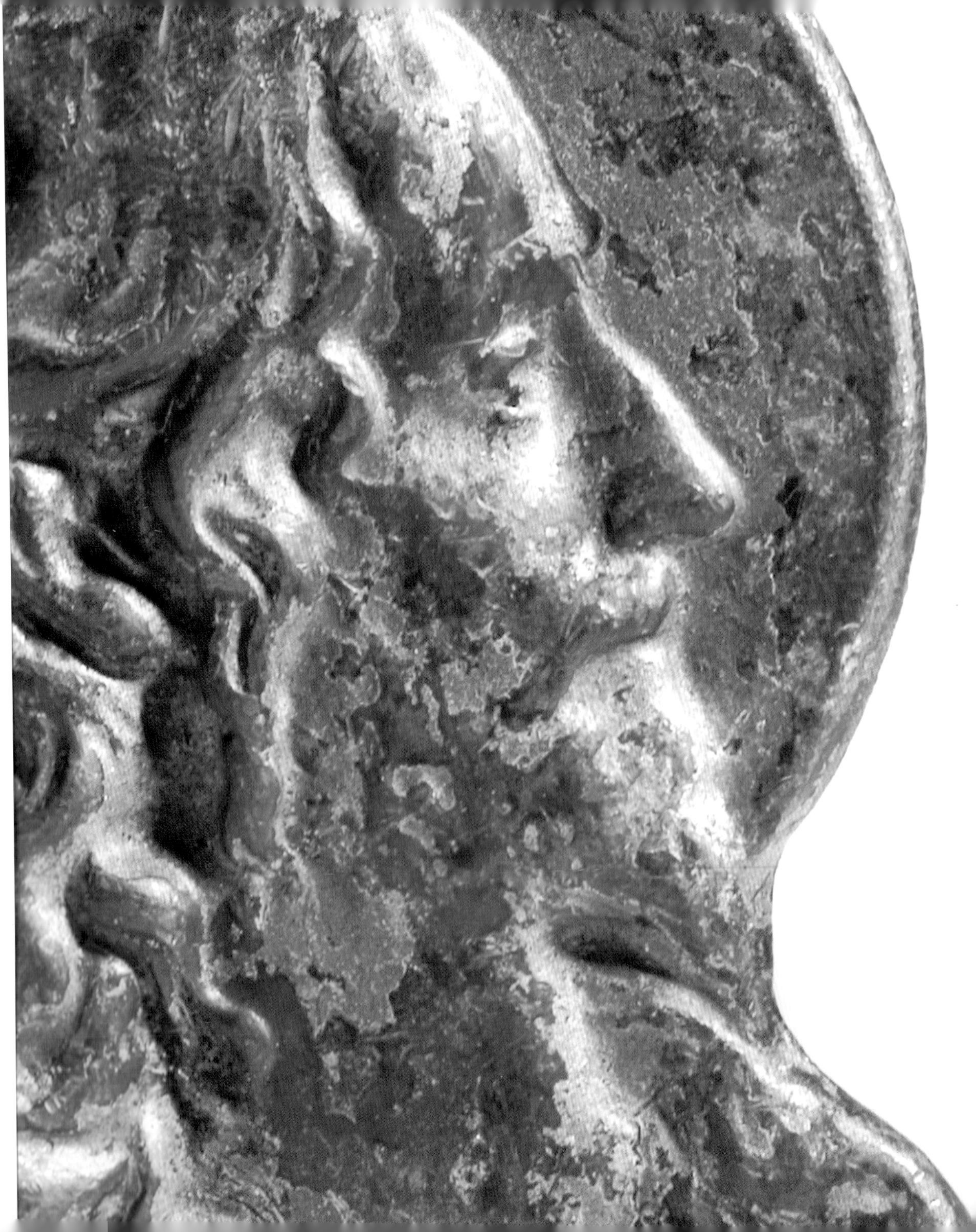

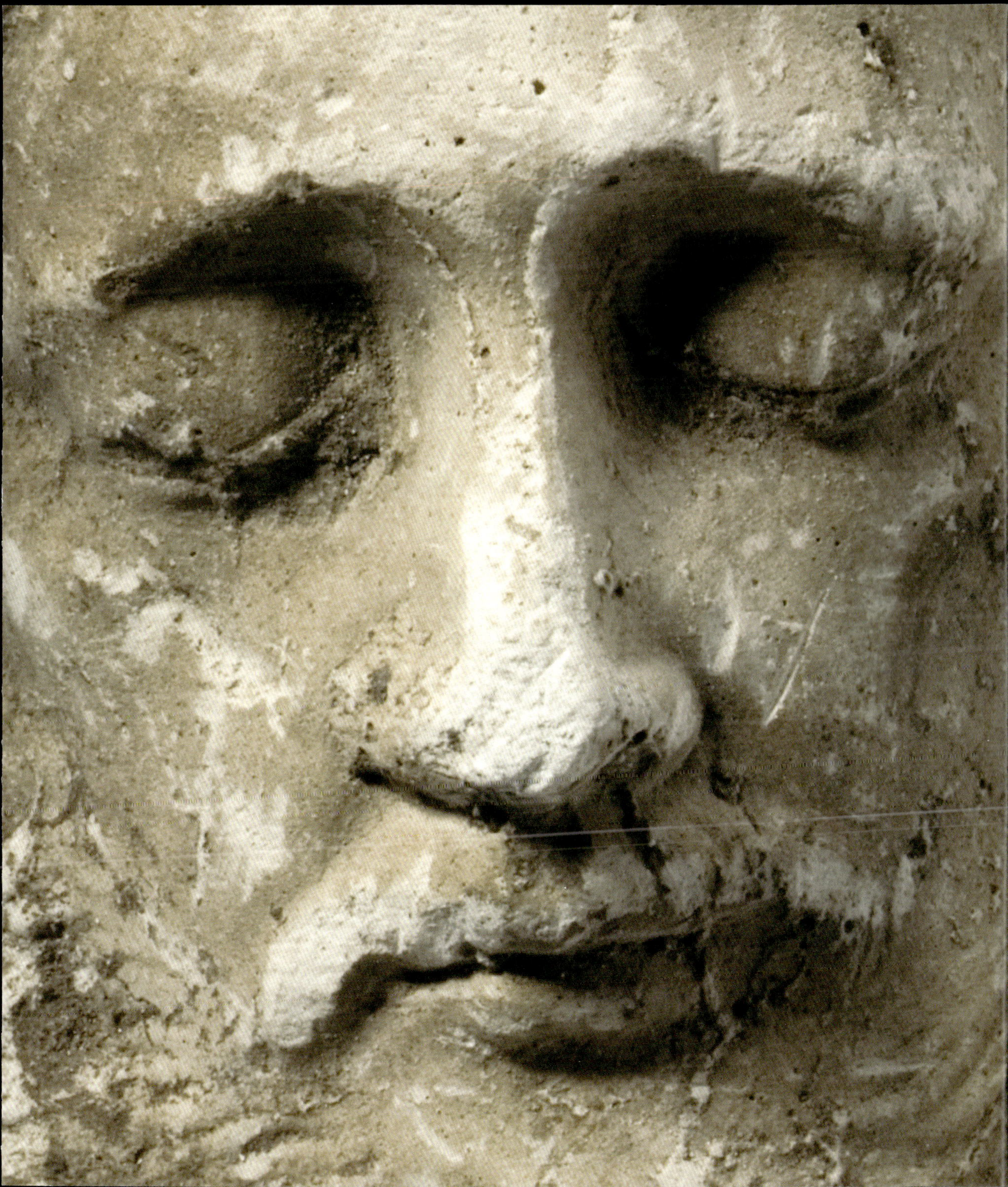

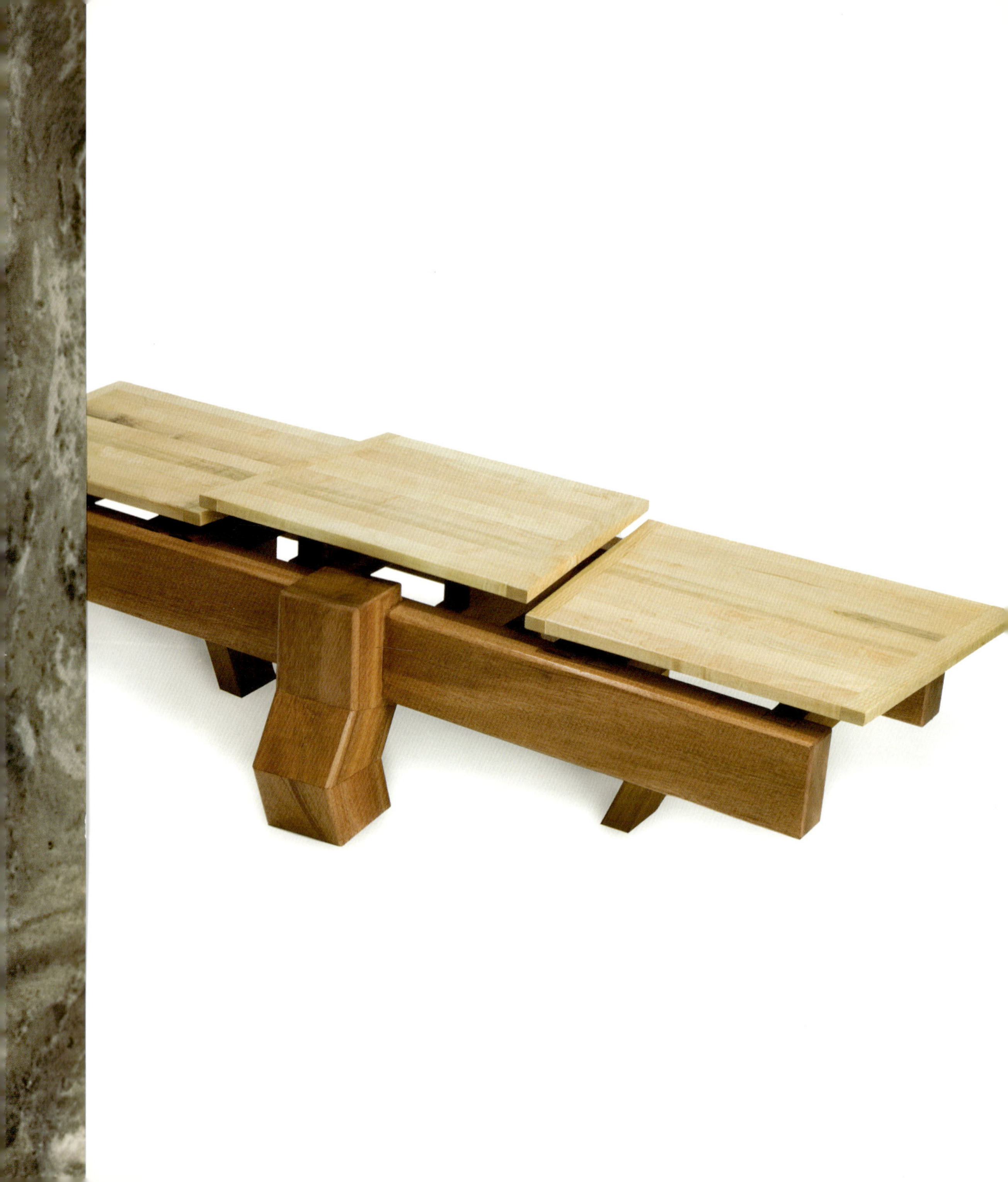

For my *Misterios* piece I designed a bench, drawing upon the structural qualities of the human body and the symbolic connotations of the cross. My choice of artifact was the headless torso of Jesus, once attached to a crucifix.

Most of my current work is technically driven, existing mostly as a display of a particular type of joinery or method of construction. This piece allowed me to free myself from certain self-imposed inhibitions and instead use simple, recognizable iconic imagery to convey a message. I intended the physical and visual weight of the piece to evoke an emotional response. Easily the largest piece I've ever built, it is also the most idea-driven, allowing me to come to terms with my views on my own Catholic upbringing. I believe my increasingly cynical religious views are due mostly to overexposure to related imagery as a young child, which had, in part, a "numbing" effect. The making process gave me an opportunity to explore these views and build something that both exalts and downplays the significance of an important religious icon, the cross.

Jason T. O'Brien

Untitled (2007)

Mahogany
Curly Maple
18″ x 72″ x 24″

Mexican tradition celebrates the lives of the departed; Victorian mores dictate a conservative, if not dour, remembrance. My inspiration for this piece comes from an interest in exploring the relationship between the two.

The artifact given to me of a deceased child's face rested in an alcove of my ceramic vessel's belly. The interior space of the form is meant to contain this child's remains, while the exterior encapsulates artifacts from the child's life meant to help people remember this loved one's stunted existence. The Victorian aesthetic of the vessel is meant to keep the piece's language formal as it communicates a difficult and sometimes uncomfortable subject matter for most. The bizarre juxtaposition of Mexican and Victorian cultures gives the piece its unique stature and power.

Mary C. O'Malley

Urn (2007)

Porcelain
21½" x 7" x 7"

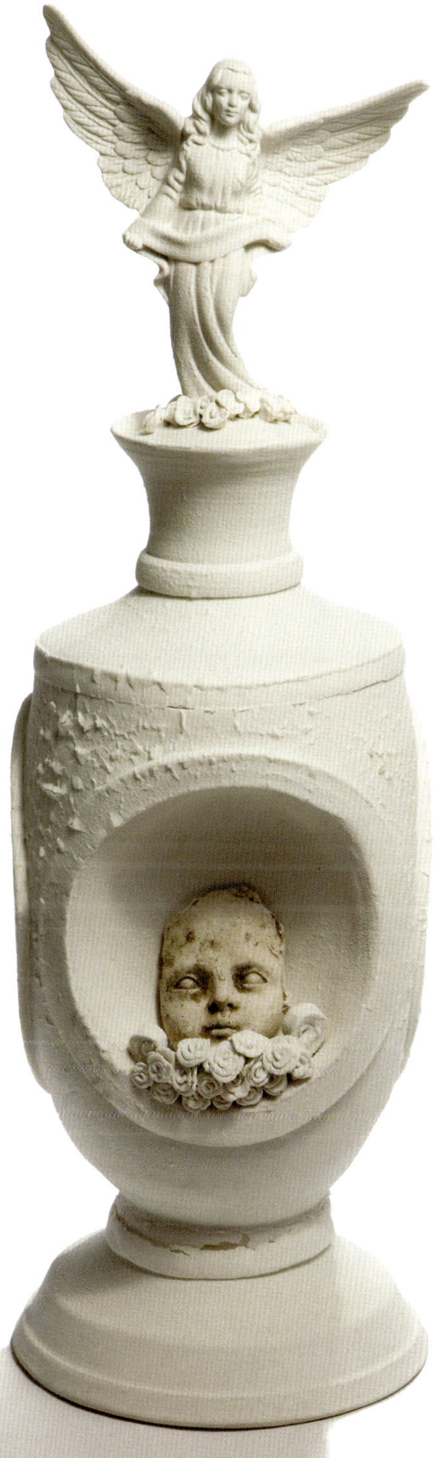

124   MISTERIOS

Amy L. Peseller

Untitled (2007)

Porcelain
Purple Fabric
Glass Droppers
various sizes

I was inspired by the Saint Mother Mary glass vase. This vase was used to contain holy water and was an inspiration to me because of its intention and function. Seeing the *Tesoros* exhibition sparked my ideas about the Catholic religion and the methods they used to worship and pray.

Just recently a woman named Patricia O'Shea (the mother of my closest friend) passed away. During her illness in the hospital, the priest from the O'Shea family's church came and blessed her body, freeing her of any sins, and allowing her soul to go to heaven. A similar blessing was again made before her funeral. This prayer is called "The Last Rights." It is a very honorable and holy ritual in the Catholic religion for one who is dying and unable to pray for forgiveness on their own.

During this prayer, the priest has a vial of blessed oils, which he uses to splash or draw a cross on the forehead. To me, the vial of oil seemed similar to the Saint Mother Mary glass vase, and that idea, along with my grief for Mrs. O'Shea, led me to create my porcelain oil vessels.

When I think of something that is meant to represent the Catholic Church, I see it as being clean and pure. I wanted my piece to encompass these characteristics, and I continued to pursue them as I threw. My small porcelain vessels have minimalist qualities, and the aura of their presentation is very serious and quiet.

I learned a great deal about using my intuitive thoughts and honoring something, or someone, abstractly and personally, instead of trying to be narrative. I took pride in my results without comparing the pros and cons to my peers. Of all the projects I created thus far as a junior at The University of the Arts, this piece means the most to me. As a wheel thrower, the oil vessels are related to my preceding works that were formed through that process and my instinct to create function. This piece was completely different, however, because of its material and structure and my ability to see through the doubt I usually have when beginning an assignment. Making this project has, for the first time, made me feel not like a student in art school but an artist.

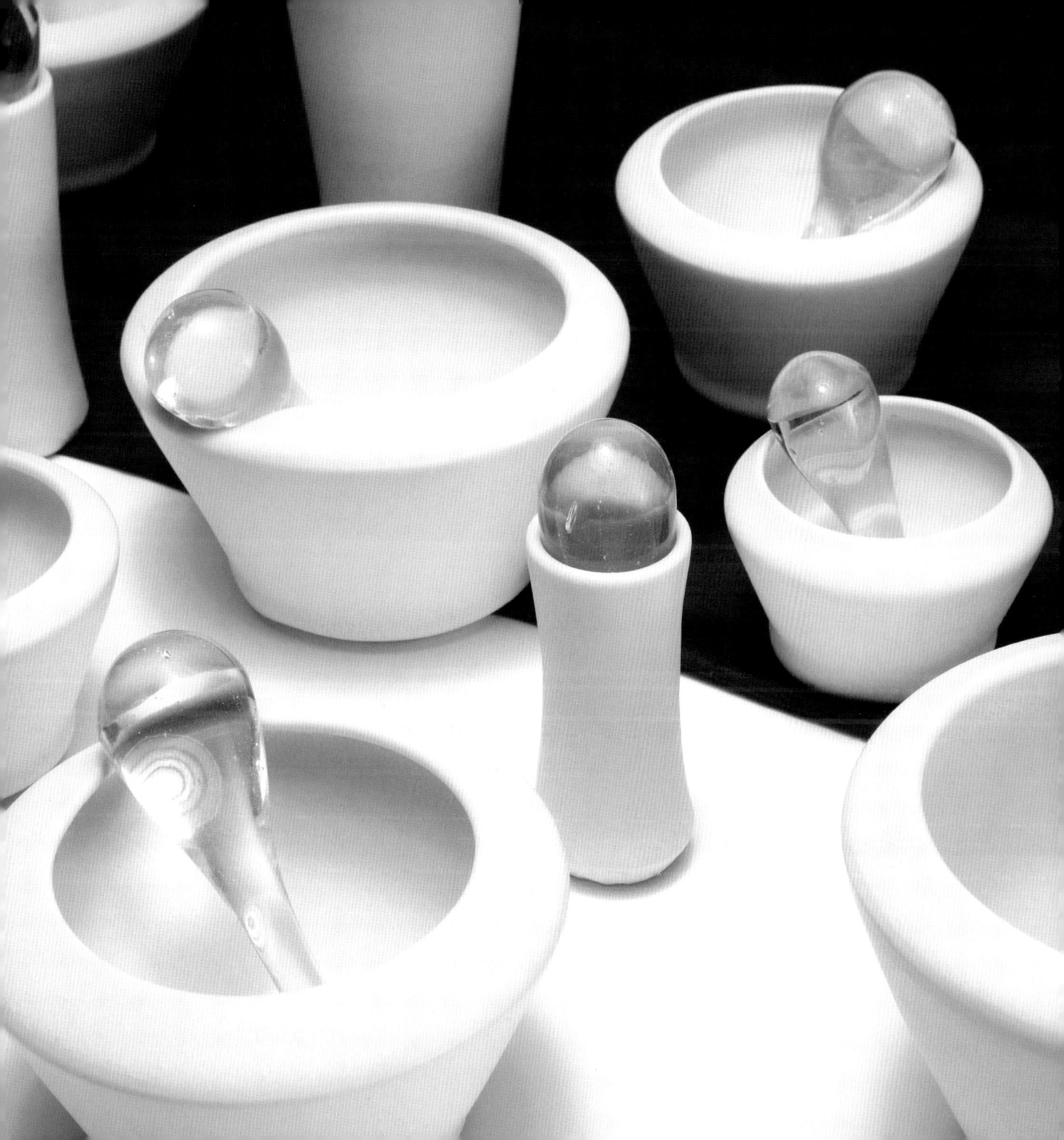

126 MISTERIOS

Joseph M. Pillari

Reliquary (2007)

Sterling Silver
Walnut
4" x 3" x 2"

God is a dead man, leaving only the good.

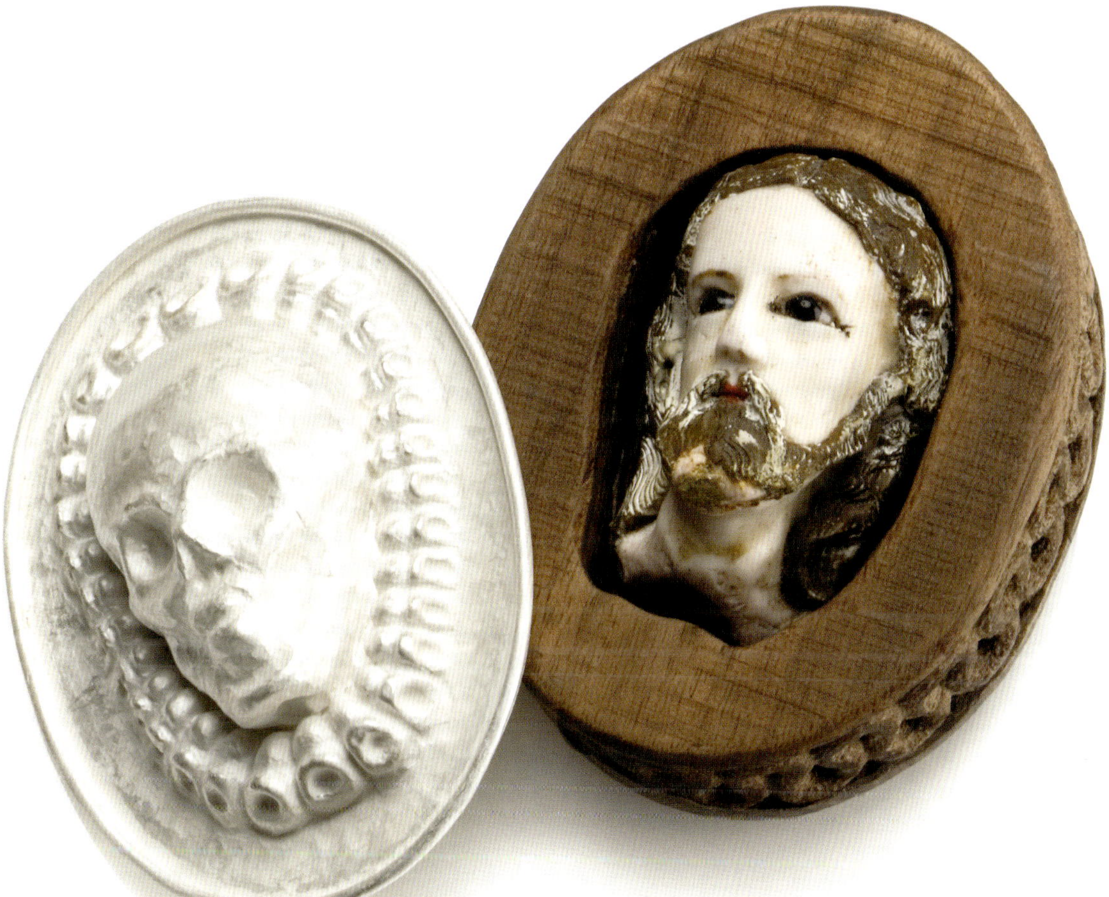

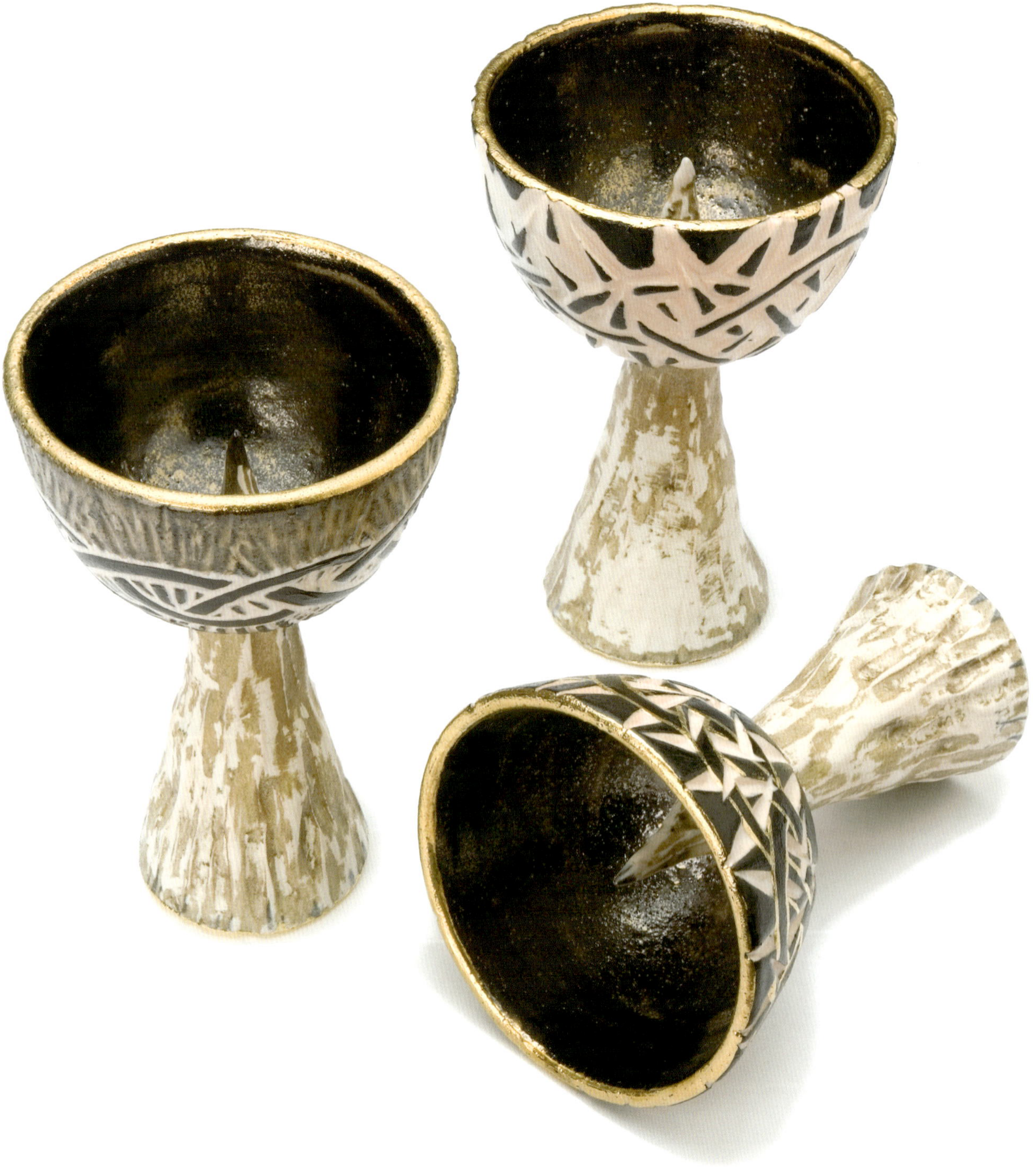

I was inspired by a carved wooden head of Jesus. The intertwined crown of thorns is both beautiful and horrible; the blood slowly trickles down Christ's wounded brow. I decided to make three ceremonial chalices based on the head to hold the Eucharistic blood of Christ. Through simple form and texture, I created an image that references the sensuous, serpentine vine and the painful, stabbing thorns. They are Christian ceremonial vessels intended to evoke emotion in the user.

Lauren P. Rider

La Sangre De Cristo (2007)

Porcelain
Black Slip
6 ½" x 4 ½" x 4 ½"

When I first saw the cherub's head, I was filled with two strong, contradictory emotions. Its soft, baby-like features made me happy, but at the same time, there was something in that sleeping face that reminded me of death. I wanted my viewers to experience this for themselves, and so I chose to draw them into a grove of silver trees that enclosed my cherub. The trees are bare, a little wistful, and refer to childhood memories of visiting my father's grave; at the same time, they create a calm haven for this cherub's peaceful rest.

Elizabeth K. Rogers

Untitled (2007)

Silver
Mirror
Wooden Artifact
10″ x 10″ x 8″

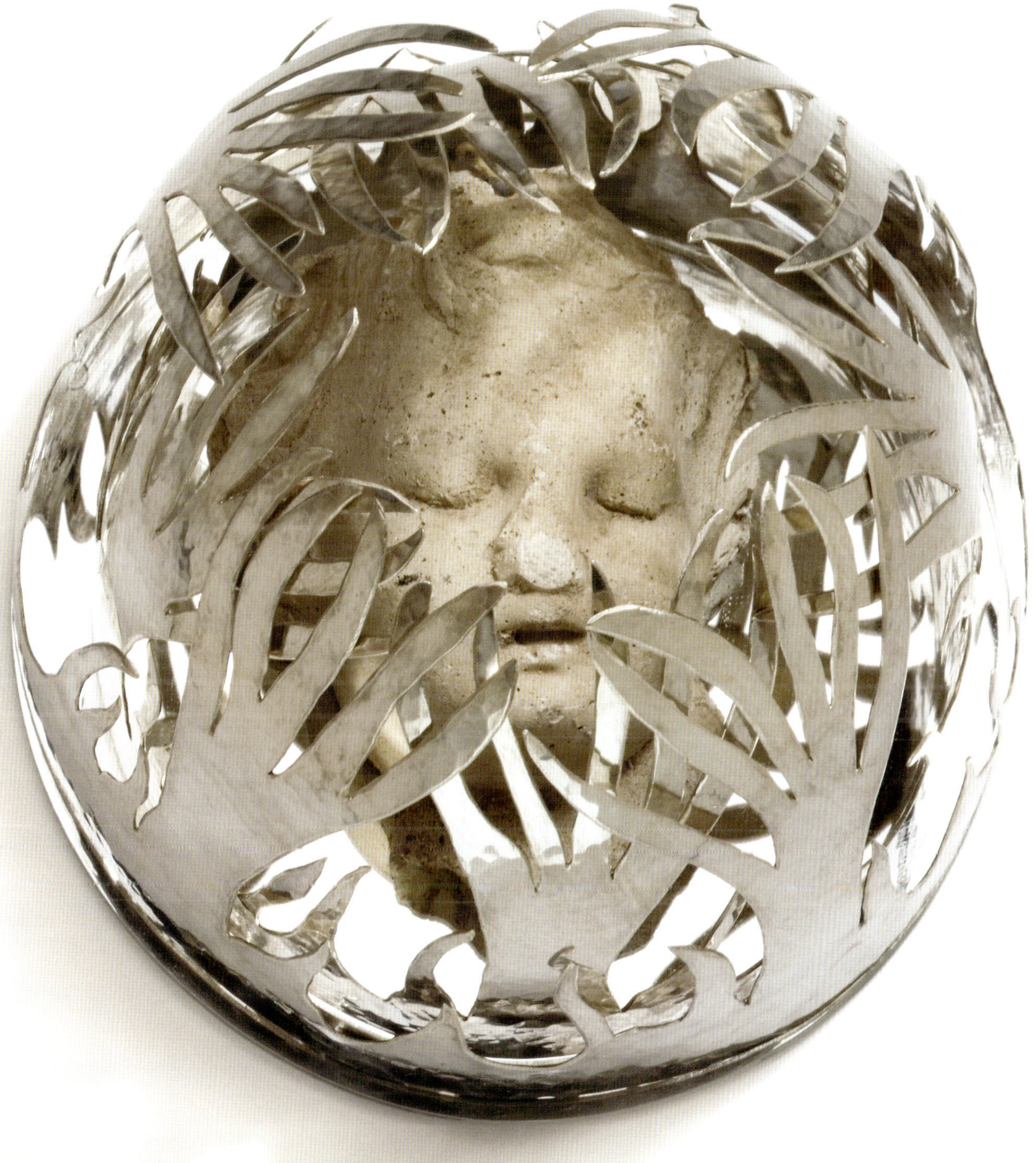

132 MISTERIOS

The colonial art and artifacts of Latin America are steeped in the Catholic faith and its imagery. While I was raised Catholic, I have studied the different religions of the world in order to better understand religion and spirituality. My inspiration for this piece is based on faith as a principle. I deeply respect all those who are truly reverent and who deeply follow their faith. This is a shrine to them, and to you, for your devotion and reverence.

Shannon E. Ryan

Untitled (2007)

Cast Glass
3" x 2" to 6" x 7" (various)

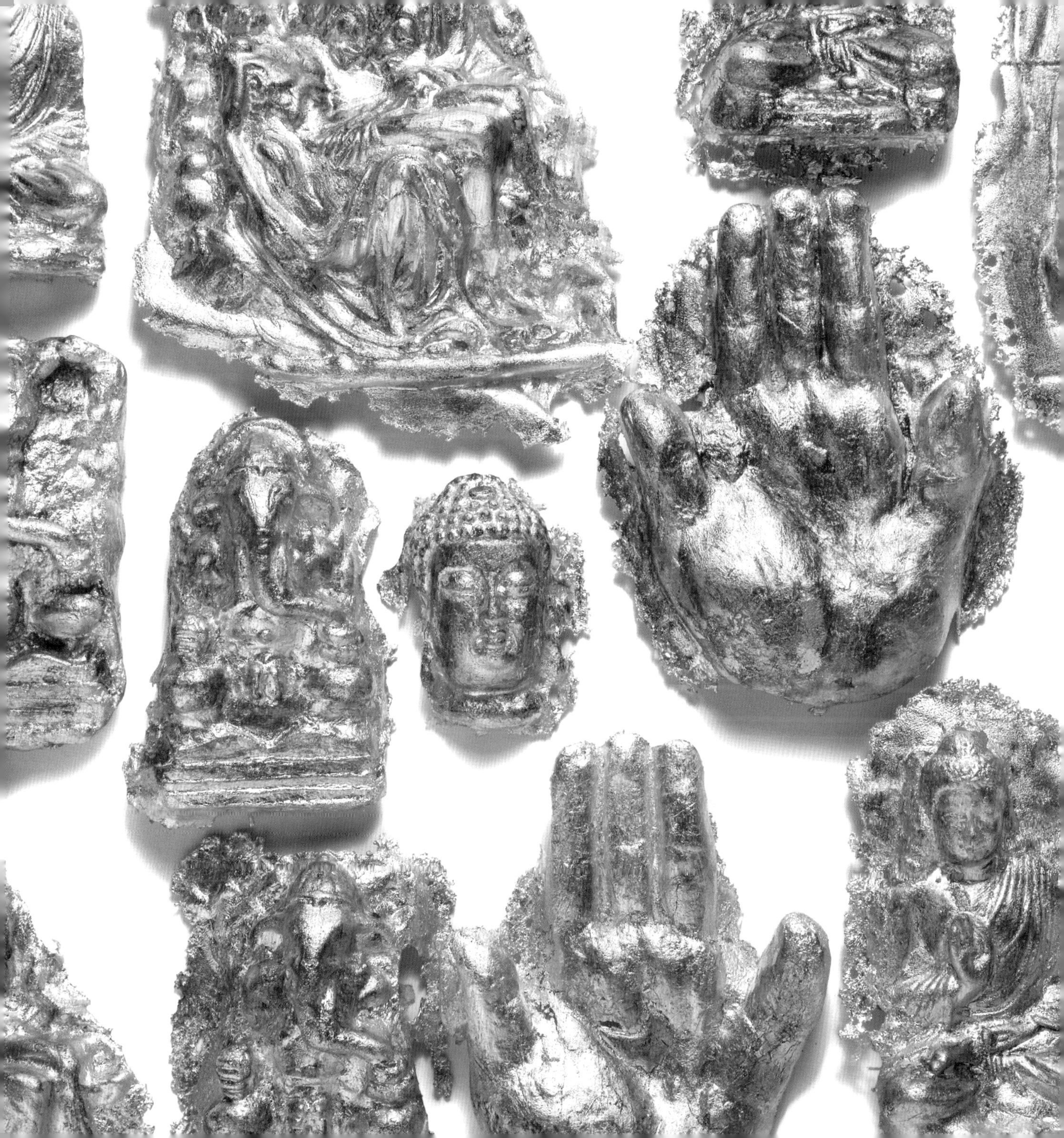

Jason S. Saul

Pure Taste (2006)

Acrylic RP Resin
Earphones
33″ x 1″ x ½″

I found the *Tesoros* exhibition and the Colonial Mexican Artifacts both confusing and frustrating. I was unable to relate to the social, cultural and religious content of either. What was presented to me as a collection of precious artifacts struck me as an assortment of cast-off objects. I did respond, however, to a ceramic fragment—a cherub's face— a piece of a sculpture with timeless beauty. After several false attempts, I decided to adapt it digitally as a piece of 21st century jewelry, a headset for my MP3 player. The digital laminated form beautifully reconstructed what sculpting and casting had previously produced. The investigation inspired by this historical "artifact" addresses contemporary concerns with authenticity, authority and the relationship between traditional and digital technologies.

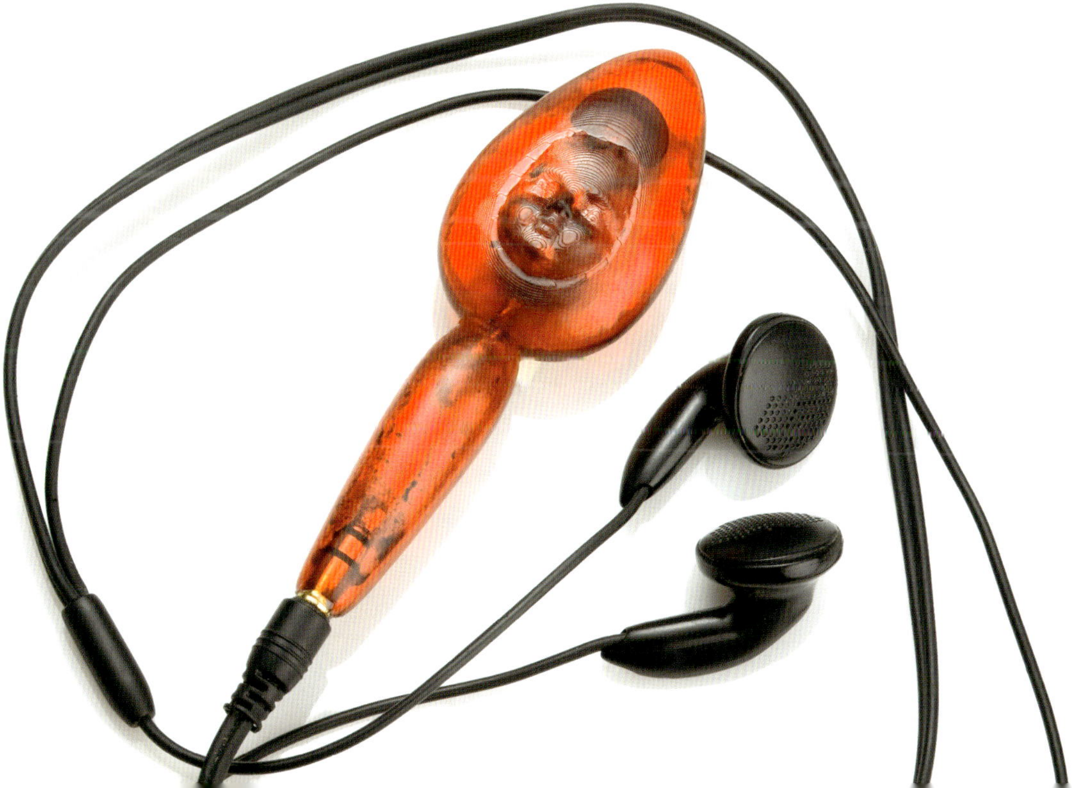

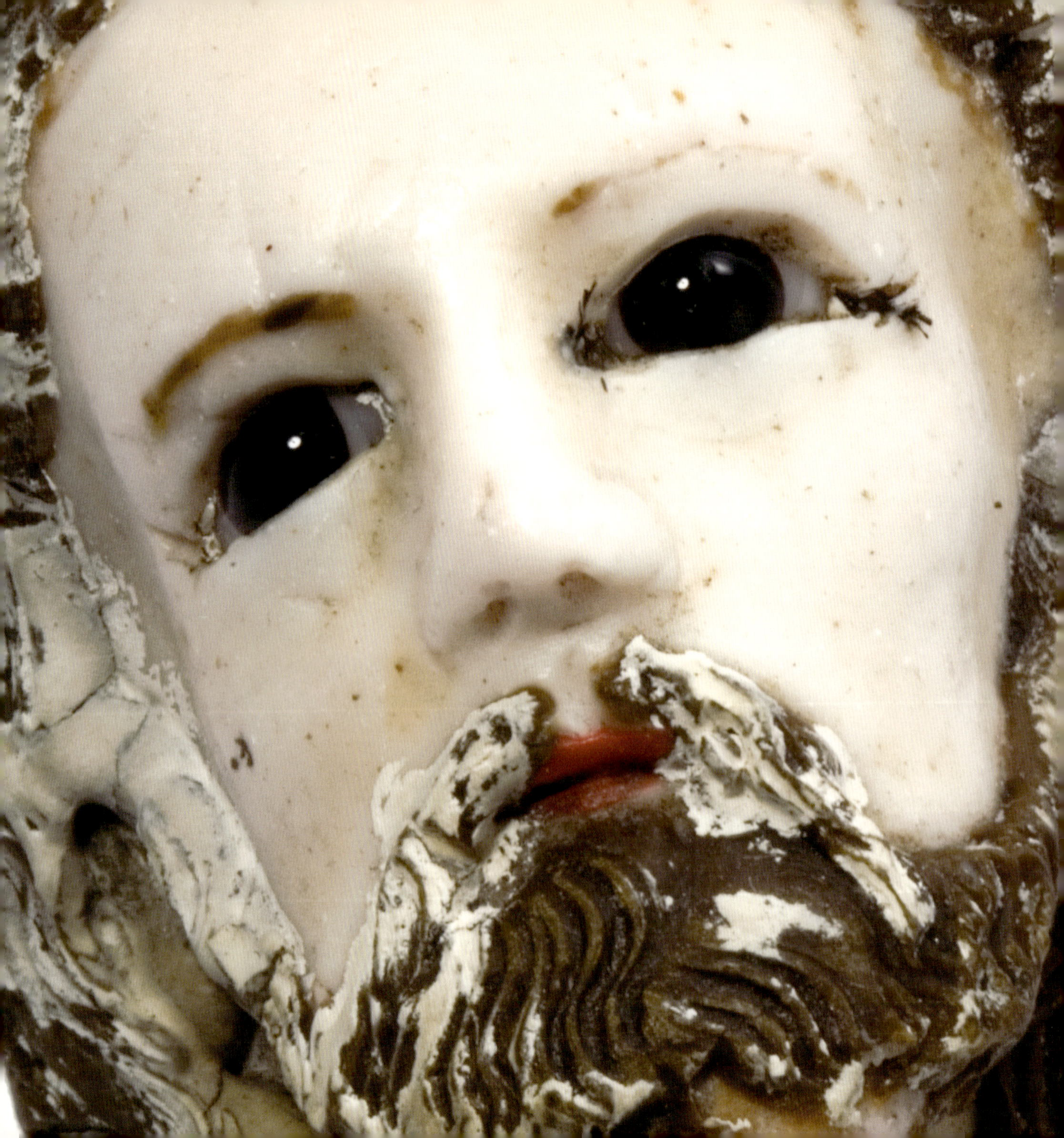

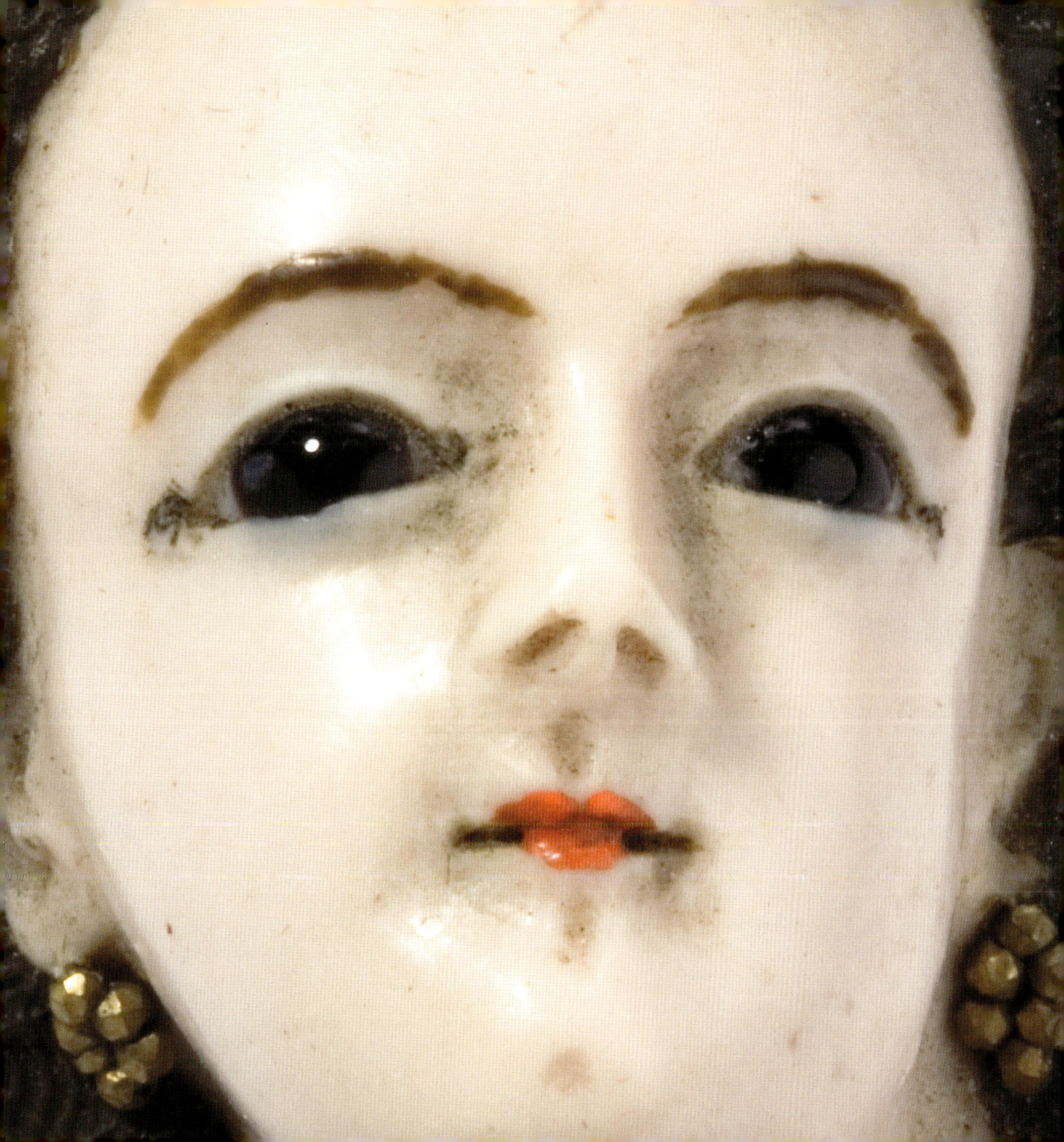

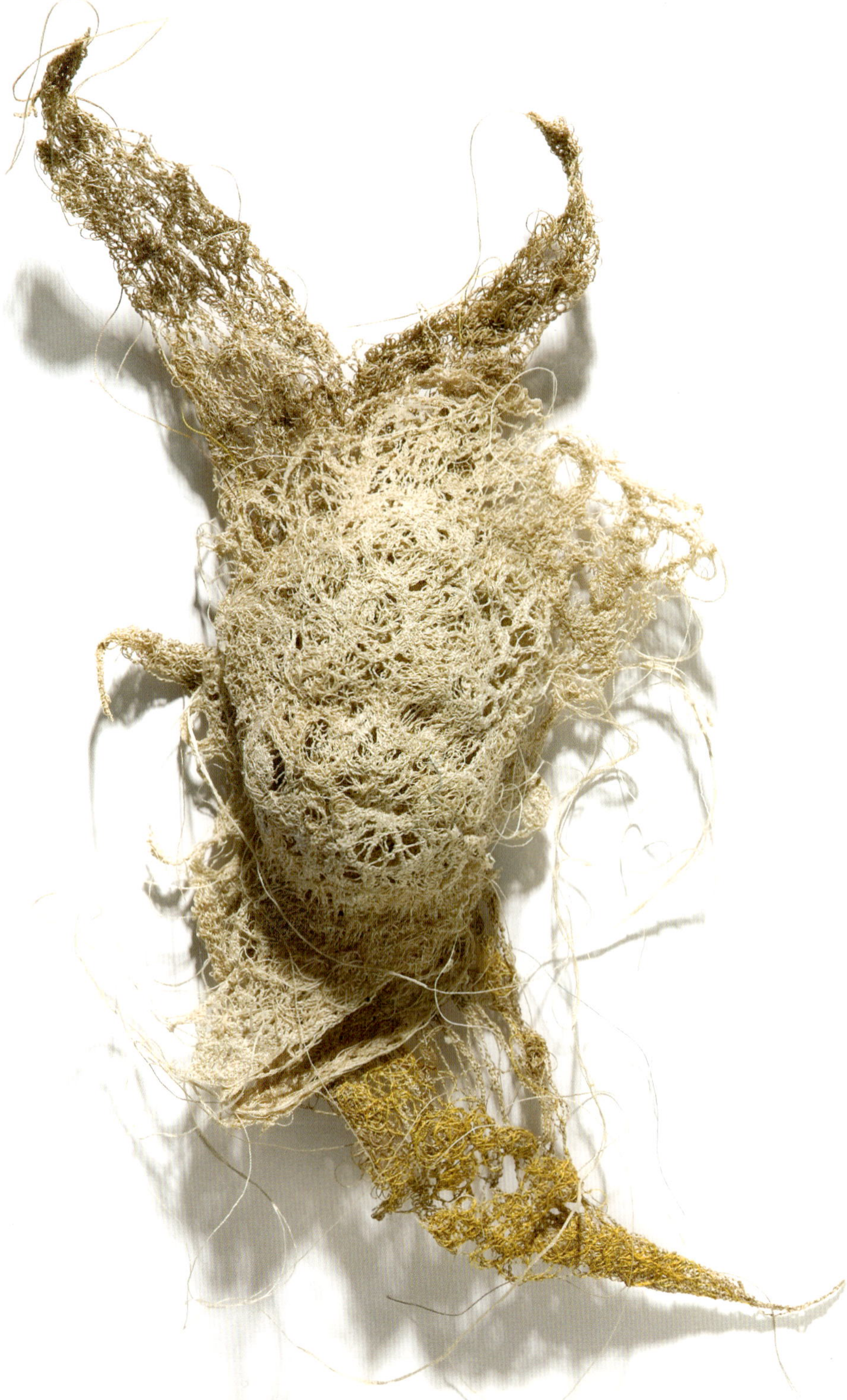

The idea of working with colonial Latin American objects initially excited me, but when presented with the actual objects, I found them so laden with their own history that they became intimidating to work with. I had to completely disassociate the plaster cherub head from its past, which allowed me to view it more objectively as a baby's head. I felt seriously overwhelmed, which forced me to retreat to my own world of making. How could I manipulate my recent experiments in lace-making to work within the context of the assignment? The final solution involved combining my experience in cast felt with what I had discovered about lace. Then I was able to create my own cast lace cherub.

Margaret J. Schreiter

Untitled (2007)

Sewing Thread
Plastic
10" x 3" x 11"

Pain, suffering and vulnerability are qualities expressed by this broken Christ figure. Over time, this wooden figure has literally been maimed and debilitated, creating a powerful and empathetic image. To me, the physical condition of this Christ figure represents how people's faith and spirituality have turned away from religious practice and towards a more narcissistic idea of God. This scaffolding supports and resurrects an icon that has fallen from grace.

Michael J. Studebaker

Reclamation (2006)

Sterling Silver
Carved Wooden Artifact
8″ x 8″ x 12″

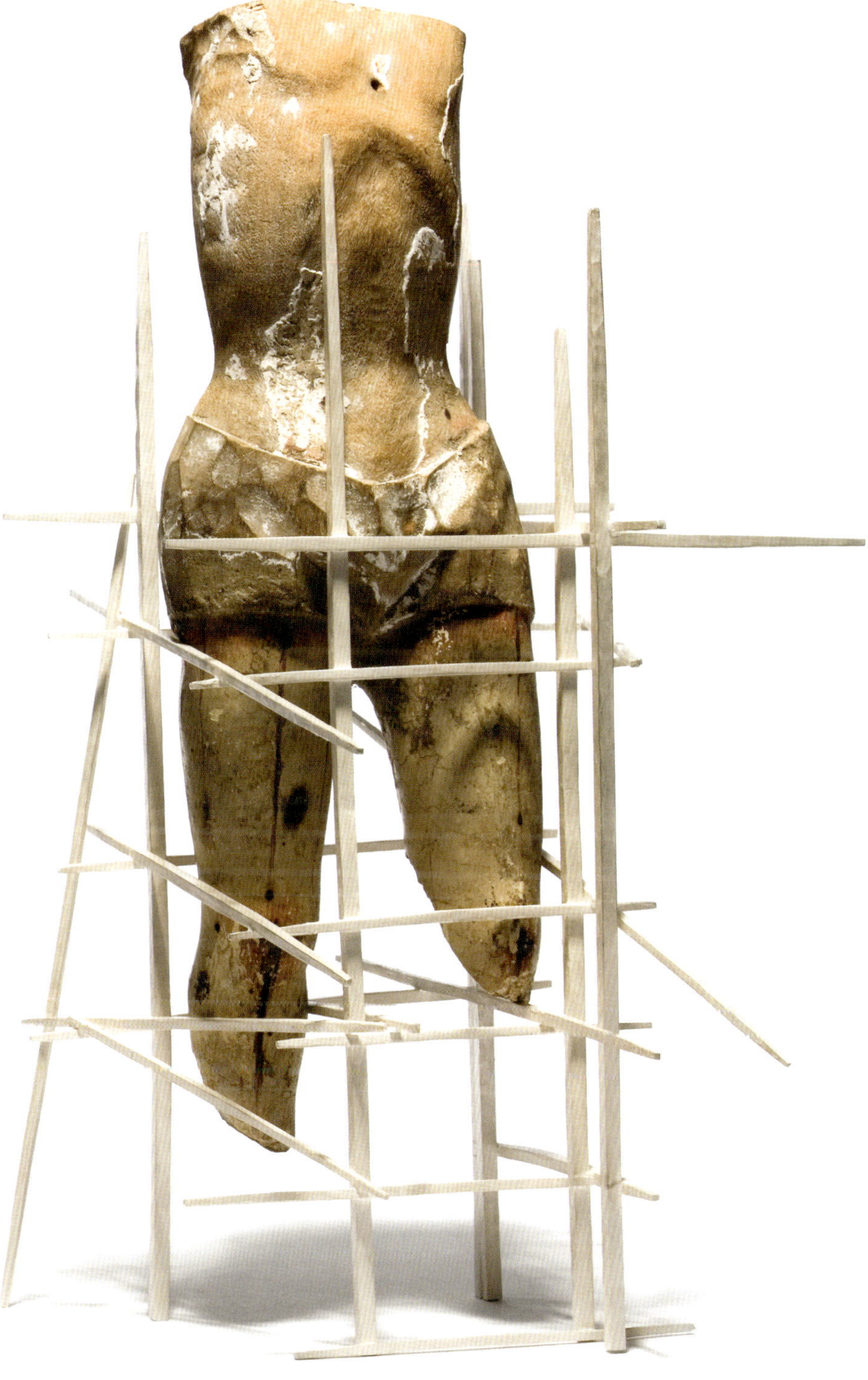

Though beautiful, there was an element of sadness in some of the religious iconography in the *Tesoros* exhibition. This struck a chord with me; I am interested in the relationship between beauty and pain or suffering. I was drawn to the milagros and the idea that these objects represent a communication with God. I was also influenced by what the artifacts represent: the need for help, hope and gratitude. This idea, along with the *Tesoros* exhibition, inspired me to create a piece that is beautiful and tells a story of survival and change.

My piece deals with the despair brought by the conquistadors and the adaptation of culture that resulted from their arrival. The Variola or Small Pox virus, brought by the Spaniards, infected large populations, making it possible for the Spaniards to conquer and christen. Etched into the pendant's back panel is an abstraction of the Variola virus, representing death, loss and defeat. The pendant's front displays a linear image of Jesus; this signifies light, power and the hope brought by religious belief.

Paola Tawa

Variola 411 (2007)

Sterling Silver
Gold Filled Wire
Resin
Car Paint
Artifact
3″ x 24″ (Entire piece)
3″ x 4½″ (Pendant only)

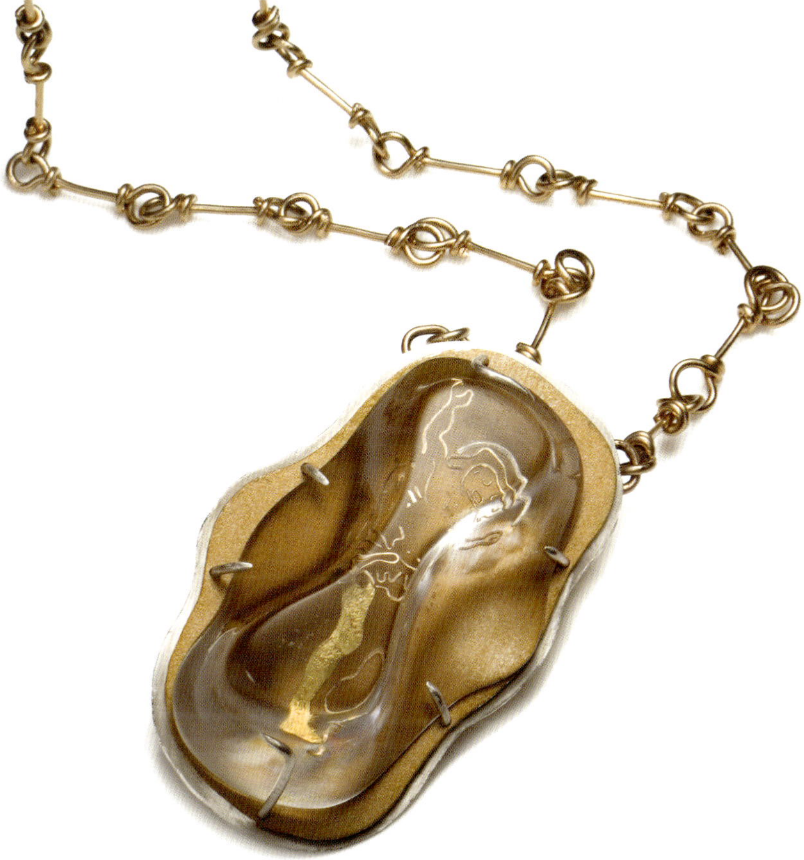

This piece is a response to a doll of the Virgin Mary. I was originally drawn to this artifact because I felt it had a strong narrative; it made me reminiscent of childhood. I was inspired by the relationship between children and their toys. A child is ultimately responsible for the fate of his or her possessions. At a time when a child has little or no control over any other life form, this ownership provides an opportunity to either destroy or embrace a weaker being. These concepts translate in adulthood to the relationships between humans and animals. Ultimately, I feel we have complete control over their welfare, and we have a similar opportunity to embrace or destroy what many consider to be weaker beings. The doll has inspired me to consider qualities of childlike curiosity, such as the way a child would act out experiments on their toys, lacking compassion or a concept of life and death. For example, as a child, I would often cut all of my Barbie doll's hair off, or tie a string around it and swing it from my bedroom window. To me, dolls and toys were living beings that could feel jealousy or sadness, yet I lacked the concept of death. I have expressed these notions on a more serious level with this piece, translating my childlike curiosity into scenes depicting the strong impact humans have over animals.

My work aims to allow the viewer to feel empathy for the subject, as does much of the sculpture in the *Tesoros* exhibition that depicts the Passion of Christ. This project has allowed me to deal with concepts I have been working with throughout the year, while giving me a new perspective on their context.

Kirsten A. Teel

Experiments in Binding (2007)

Porcelain
Coated String
16" x 18" x 22"

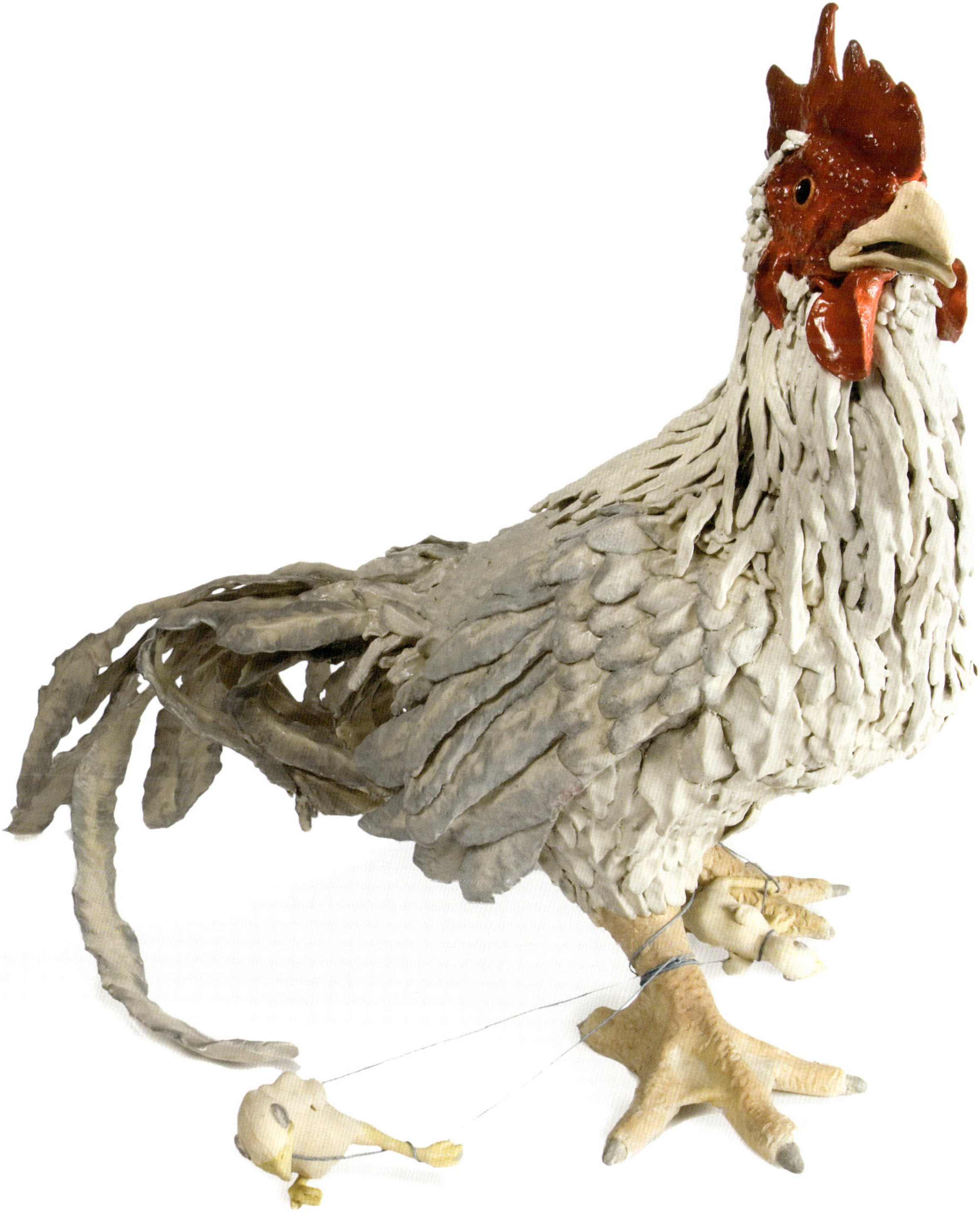

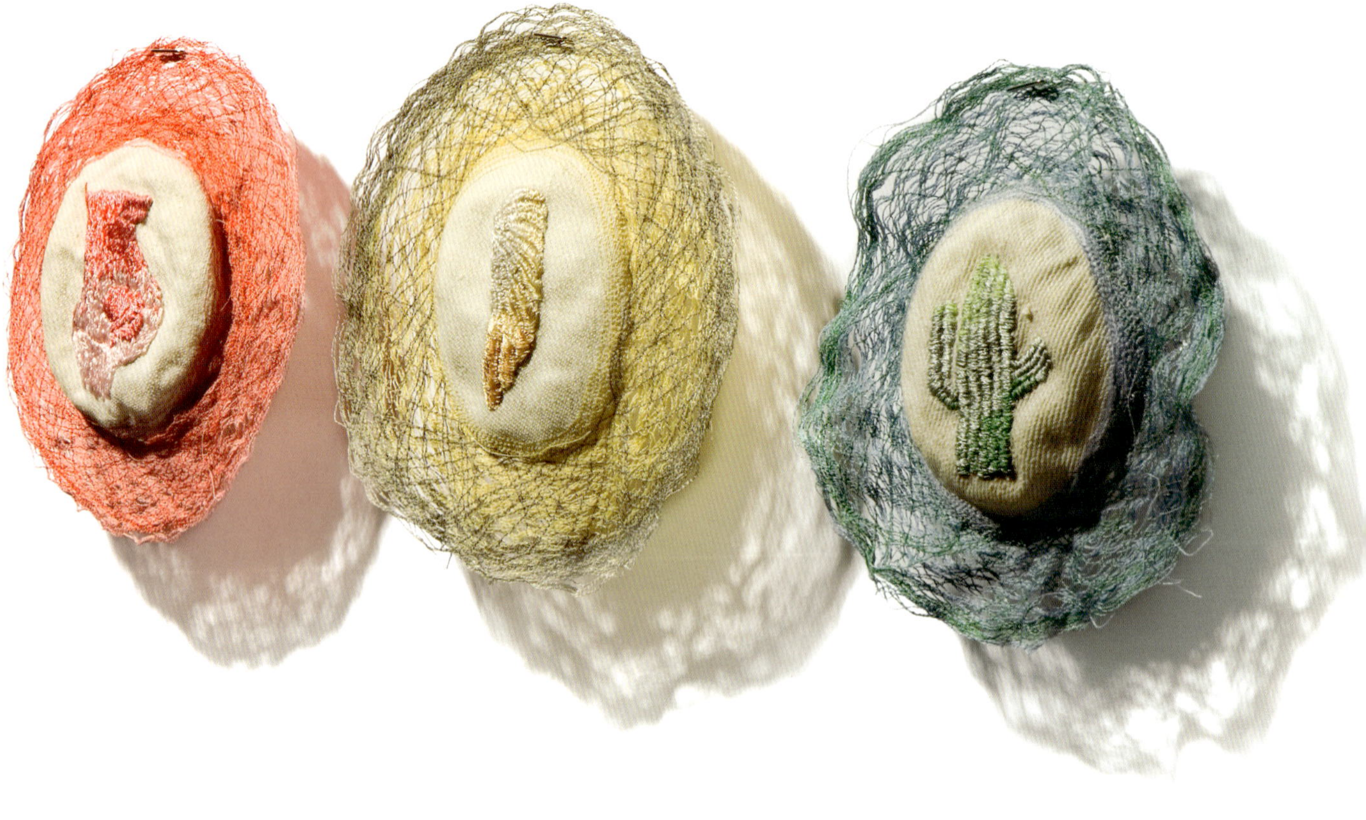

Chia-Wei Ting

Baby's Needs (2006)

Sewing Threads
Embroidery Threads
Canvas
6″ diameter (pink and green pieces)
7″ diameter (yellow piece)

I am drawn to the clay baby face; it makes me feel lost and out of place. It makes me feel sad, and I want to help this poor baby. In response to the artifact, I have created three wall pieces. The processes I have used are hand embroidery and machine stitching. The images are the things my baby angel face is missing: wings, a home and a mother. My other work uses similar means of expression; I often use irregular lines, joyous colors and simple, childlike drawing. This experience has affected the way I consider and observe things.

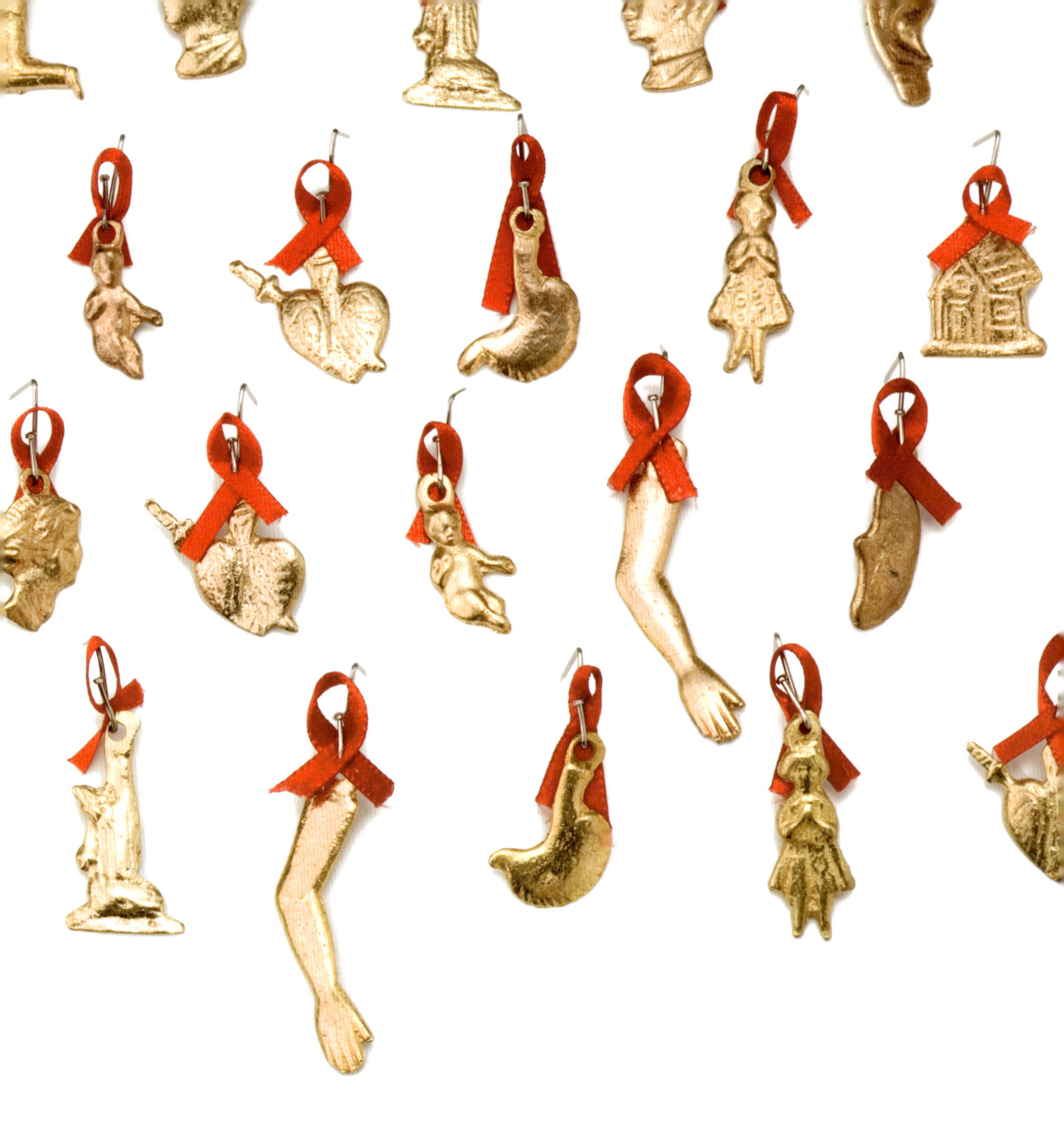

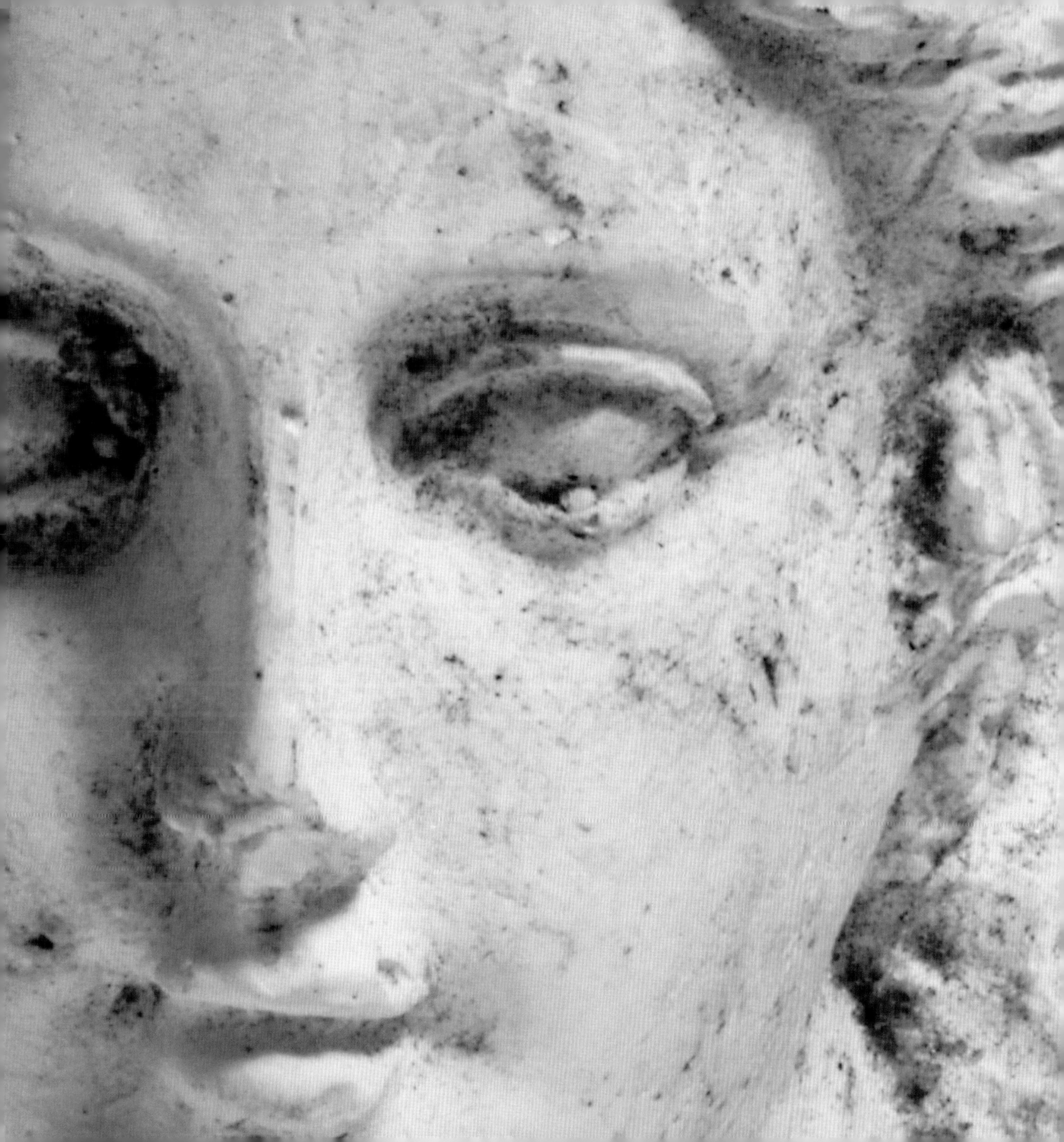

"Angelito, a Mourning Portrait" is my interpretation of a traditional piece of mourning jewelry. When children are subjects of funerary portraits, they are often depicted as little angels; in Mexico they are known as "angelitos." The life of a child is so precious that its death is horrific. This is why I chose to replicate a plaster cherub face to depict death. There is a fragility about the small face, lovingly held in its setting like a precious gem, that evokes the feeling of an ephemeral life.

I used a 3-D laser scanner to digitally replicate the plaster cherub face and then miniaturized the form using computer software. I then made a 3-D print of this form in plastic resin. Next, this tiny resin face was electroformed in copper, after which the resin was removed, leaving a copper shell to enamel on. By carefully sifting and fusing glass enamel onto this metal, I was able to work like a painter, using subtle color to capture the feeling of life slowly fading out of his face.

Stephanie L. Tomczak

Angelito, A Mourning Portrait No. 1 (2006)

Sterling Silver
Electroformed Copper
Enamel
18K Gold
Gold Leaf
1¾" x 1" x ½"

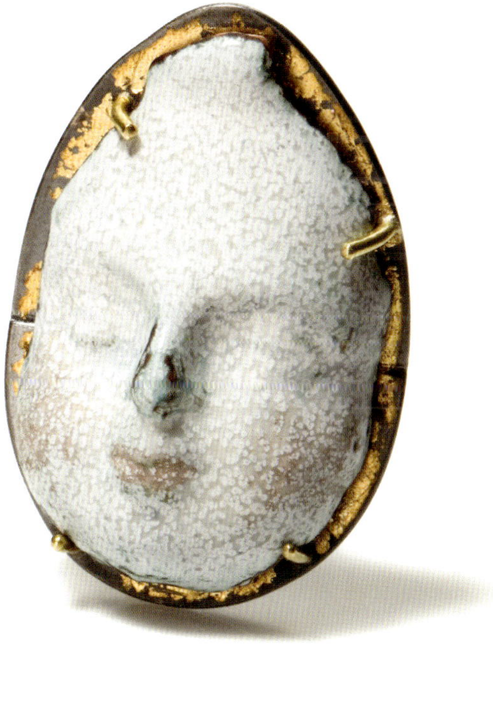

As a young girl I attended a Byzantine Catholic school. I went to church every day before school, on Sundays, and on every holy day of obligation. I was fascinated with the church's lavish interior, filled with incredible ornaments and objects of worship. Everything seemed so rich; in comparison, my father's Protestant church seemed boring.

For this project I decided to create an altar similar to the one from my memorable church-going days. I chose the cast lead portrait as my inspiration because it reminded me of some of the objects and imagery that covered the surface of that Byzantine church: reliquaries holding fragments of saints, the baptismal font, jewel-studded books, murals, etc.

I think fondly of these things and the beliefs I used to have. I sought to physically embody these memories by making a Prie Dieu that strongly references the one from my youth.

Marcy Vanderburg

Exaltation (2006)

Mahogany
Purple Heart
Upholstery
Runner
Lead and Brass Icon (Artifact)
28" x 14" x 32"

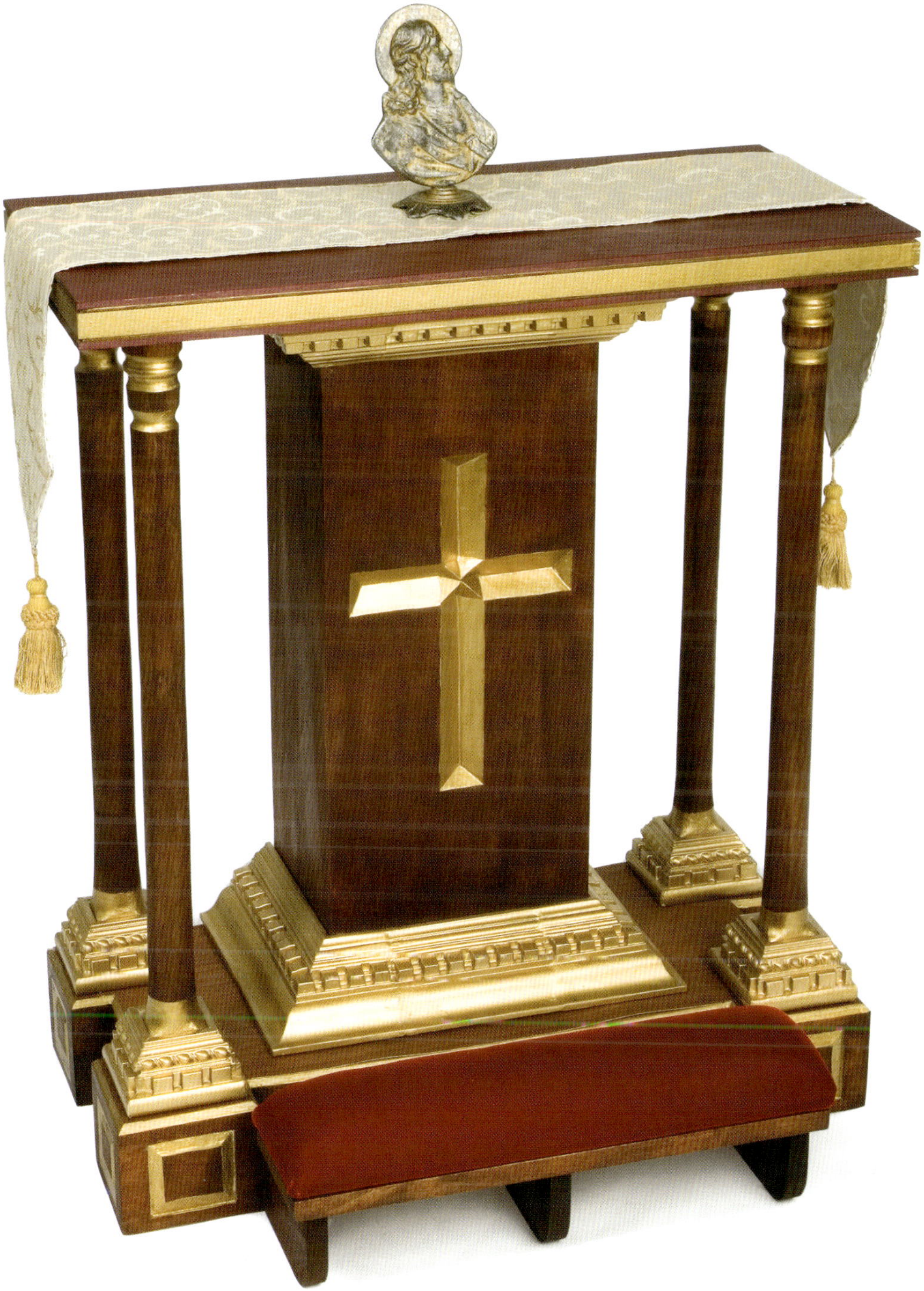

Kort A. Walsh

Acanthus Variation 1 (2007)

Copper
Bronze
Silver
Steel
3¼" x 2½"

The large, heavy and highly decorated cast brass frame was particularly interesting to me because it was one of the few artifacts that was purely decorative. Studying that decoration and mixing it with my thoughts on *Tesoros*, I chose to work with the image of a single leaf and make a brooch that is fully expressive of the baroque artwork of colonial Mexico.

The *Tesoros* exhibition showed me a world where assimilation occurred at a bloody level. The colonial decorations in that show encouraged me to exaggerate the leaf figure, as some of the local craftsmen might have done three hundred years ago.

Working on this project has expanded my appreciation of Latin American art and my understanding of the violent cultural mix that led to such rich art.

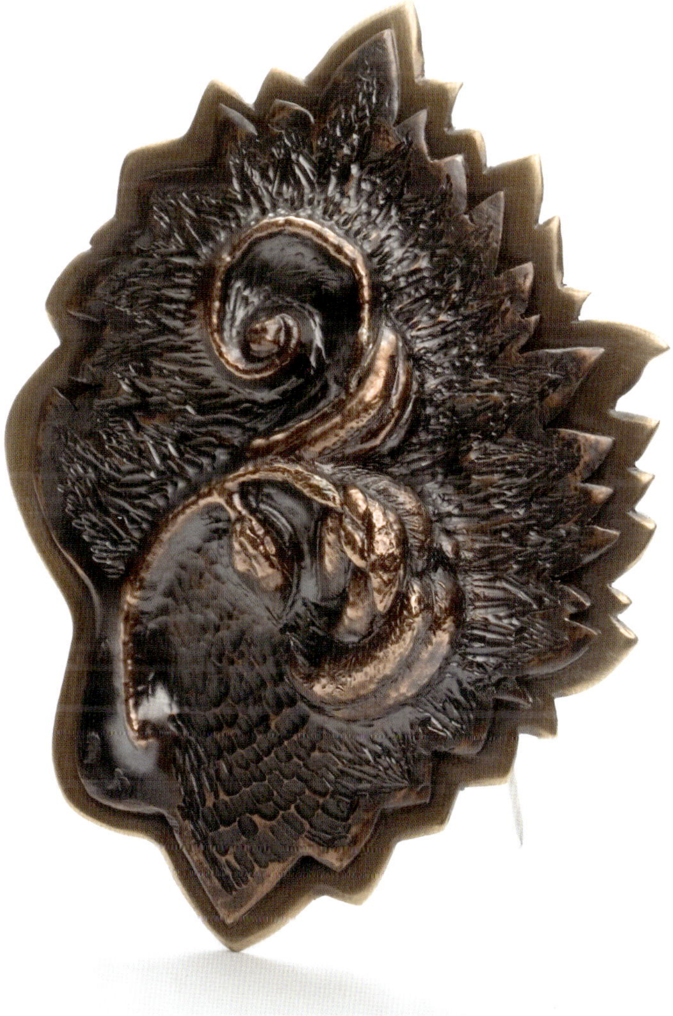

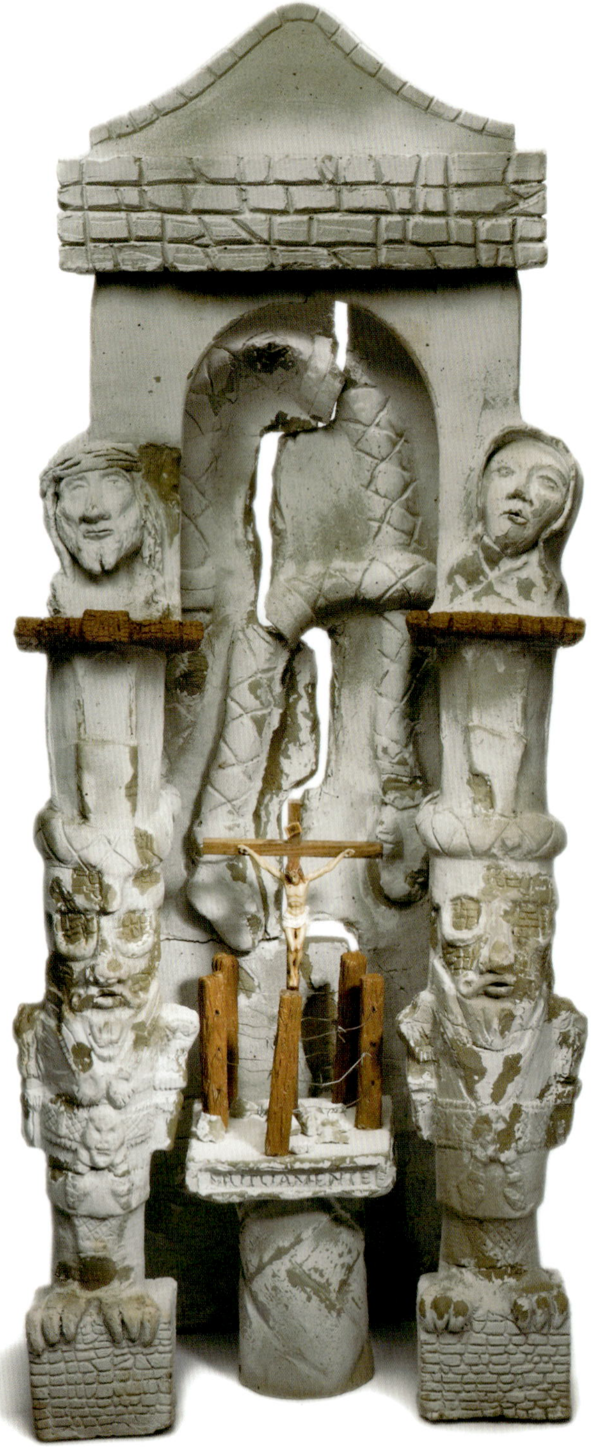

In the United States, the world of legal citizens is supported by the silhouetted world of illegal aliens, those immigrants often working in the shadows at jobs no American would want. When I viewed the *Tesoros* exhibition, this issue instantly came to my mind, and I knew that this would be the focus of my project. At the exhibit, I noticed the interweaving of ancient native culture with the symbols of Christianity. It seemed as though mutuality of the two cultures was essential to sustain a sense of native heritage.

The illegal immigrant and border issue is a major conflict in our nation. I am aware that there are many complexities to the immigration issue, but to me it seems that we could spend lots of money to build a giant fence or we can try to build relationships of mutuality and co-existence. We need to realize that the immigrants are not stealing from us, but rather giving to us. Once our nation is aware of this, we can start healing the breach that currently exists between our nations and close the rift between those who live here and those who so desperately want to.

Christopher N. Yoos

Shrine (2007)

Earthenware
36" x 18"

A cherub's face served as the inspiration for my project. A cherub is a member of an order of angels that represent the all-seeing presence of God. To me, the description of cherubs in the Bible is gruesome. The Bible describes cherubs as confrontational beasts with two pairs of wings (one for flying, one to cover them), hooved feet, and four faces: an ox, a human, a lion, and an eagle. This is a huge contrast to the plump, flying babies that became the cherubs of Late Christian Art!

As a child who was raised Catholic, I decided that stereotypical cherub imagery does not express the creepiness I felt as a child in church. I wanted to make an abstraction of the cherub described in the Bible. To do so, I reconsidered my process and technique, as well as my interest in function, sensuality and beauty. My cherub for *Misterios* became an abstract, anthropomorphic form with a confrontational aura. I used tools to rough up the clay until it looked ragged, then applied red and black iron oxide glaze to color the piece. My angel has a worn and dirty look—my darker version of a cherub, the cherub of my mind.

Lindsey A. Zmroczek

Kirubu (2007)

Stoneware
10½" x 21" x 6"

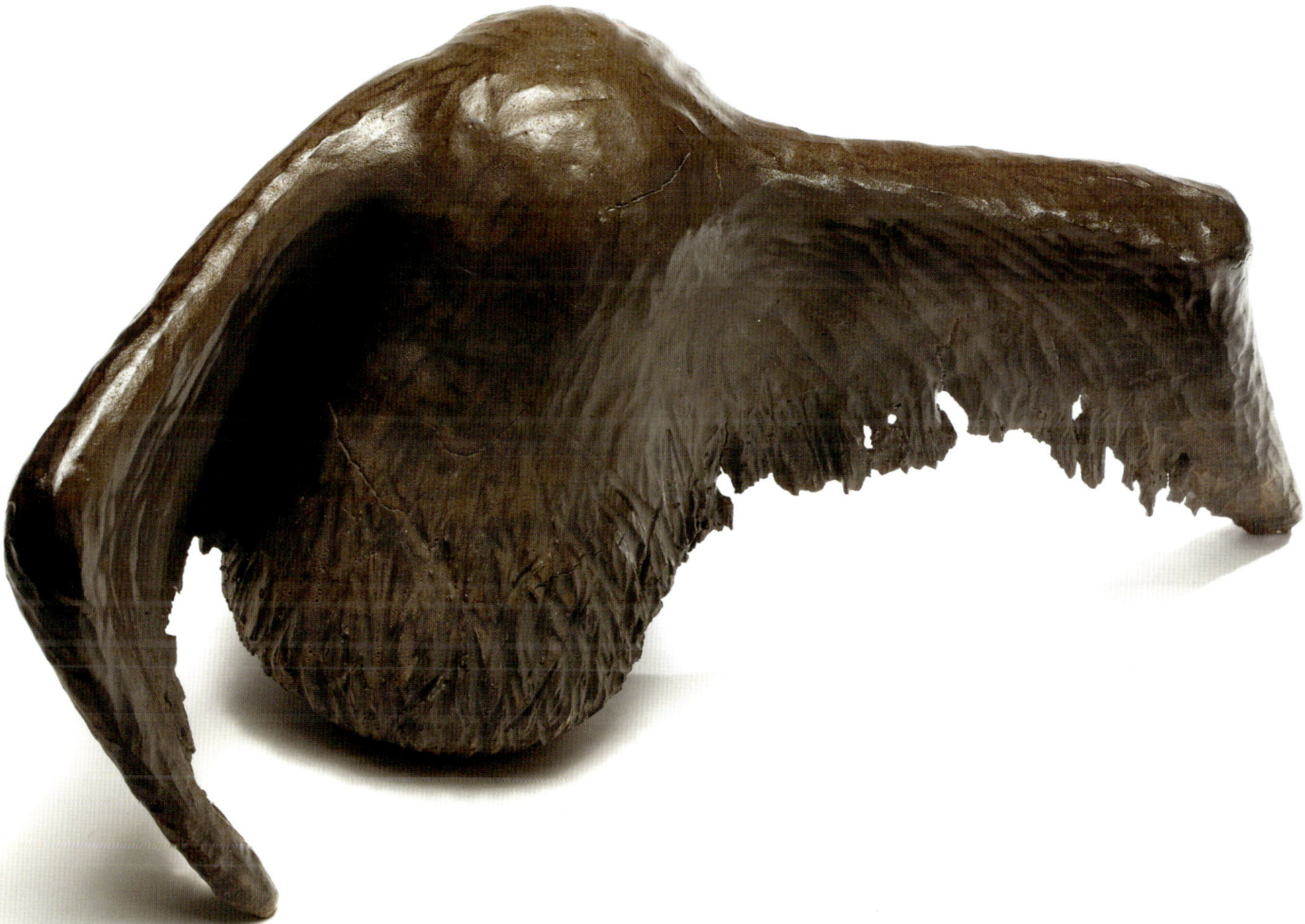

Faculty

We are deeply indebted to The University of the Arts crafts faculty for their tireless efforts in making this project a reality and for their profound devotion to their students.

ROD MCCORMICK
Chairperson, Crafts Department

Project Faculty
Sharon Church, Professor
Mi-Kyoung Lee, Assistant Professor
Don Miller, Assistant Professor
Lizbeth Stewart, Professor
Walter Zimmerman, Assistant Professor
Lola Brooks, Senior Lecturer
Heather Mae Erickson, Lecturer
Alec Karros, Adjunct Associate Professor
Judith Schaechter, Adjunct Professor

Photography
Ken Yanoviak, Senior Lecturer
Media Arts Department